If Satan Can't Steal Your Dreams...

He Can't Control Your Destiny

by
Jerry Savelle

HARRISON HOUSE
Tulsa, Oklahoma

07 06 05   10 9 8 7 6 5 4

If Satan Can't Steal Your Dreams...
He Can't Control Your Destiny
ISBN 1-57794-481-X
Copyright © 2004 by Jerry Savelle
P.O. Box 748
Crowley, Texas 76036

Published by Harrison House, Inc.
P.O. Box 35035
Tulsa, Oklahoma 74135

Contents

1
Satan Targets Your Dreams

It would be wonderful if God just laid out the whole picture of your life and said, "Now, here's where you're going; here's everything that's going to happen before you get there; here's each day of your life for the next fifteen years; and here's how it's going to turn out." However, if He did that, our lives wouldn't require faith.

God is not going to lay everything out for you. He'll give you one piece of the puzzle at a time. Each piece connected to the other piece will create a perfect picture of God's plan for your life. But those pieces must be connected together by faith in His Word. Every step you take must be a step of faith.

Psalm 37:23 says, "The steps of a good man are ordered by the Lord...." In this journey of faith, you're going to have to be very sensitive to God. Like Abraham, you must take the steps God ordains and directs so you'll end up at the destination to which He has called you.

> *By faith he* [Abraham] *sojourned in the land of promise, as in a strange country, dwelling in tabernacles with Isaac and Jacob, the heirs with him of the same promise:*
>
> *For he looked for a city which hath foundations, whose builder and maker is God.*

Hebrews 11:9,10

As you will see later in this book, Abraham didn't know where he was going, but he was always looking. Are you looking today? Are you looking for the manifestations of what God has promised? Are you anticipating the fulfillment? Are you laying aside all doubts and expecting God's every promise to happen? Right now, God is building something in your life. It is your job to look for what is built and made by God. In order to do this, you have to create a proper atmosphere and refuse to fear anything that would stand in your way—even failure.

CREATING AN ATMOSPHERE FOR YOUR DREAMS

There are things you can do to create a proper atmosphere for your dream, and there are also things that will create an improper atmosphere. What kind of atmosphere do you live in? Is there an atmosphere of faith? Is there an atmosphere of trust and belief? If so, then you will attract miracles, because faith moves God. While fear activates the adversary, faith activates God.

The Bible says that without faith it is impossible to please God. (Heb. 11:6.) Therefore, a faith atmosphere causes our God-given dreams to come to pass. A fear atmosphere only hinders them. Our dreams are fulfilled by faith.

Usually, however, the thing many people fear in life the most is failure. They fear that if they step out in their dreams, everything will fall apart.

Even if it looks as if your manifestation will never come to pass, you must allow faith and confidence to rise up within you. You must have a resolve to depend on and have faith in God alone—even if there is opposition. Micah faced such opposition, but take a look at his declaration when he faced it:

> *Therefore I will look unto the Lord; I will wait for the God of my salvation: my God will hear me.*
>
> *Rejoice not against me, O mine enemy: when I fall, I shall arise; when I sit in darkness, the Lord shall be a light unto me.*

Micah 7:7,8

"I will look unto the Lord. I will wait for the God of my salvation. My God will hear me." That's how

God wants His children to speak. God always rejoices with you when you show the confidence to overcome adversity.

Satan is the one who rejoices *against* you, especially when you make mistakes. However, when he tries to get you to wallow in self-doubt, remember this: No one is without mistake. We've all stumbled. We've all fallen at some time or another. In fact, you probably will make a few more mistakes along the way. You have to remember it's not failure to fall. It's only failure to stay down.

Micah said, "...when I fall, I shall arise...." There will come a place and a time in your life when you finally have to decide once and for all that if you fall, you will arise again no matter how far you have fallen.

Look at what the Bible says in Psalm 37:23-24.

The steps of a good man are ordered by the Lord: and he delighteth in his way.

Though he fall, he shall not be utterly cast down: for the Lord upholdeth him with his hand.

The devil expects you to quit. He wants you to say, "Where is God?" He wants you to get discouraged and fearful of stepping out into the biggest dreams and desires of your life. He wants you to be afraid of failure.

However, God wants you to get it into your spirit that if you fall, it is not over. He wants you to determine that no matter how many times you fall, with the support of His hand, you shall arise.

All of us have dreams and desires that we would like to see happen in our lives. Yet it seems as if all of the things we desire from God are beyond our natural ability to accomplish.

You are about to learn some life-changing principles that will help to propel you into all that you are to be. I want to help you to recapture the dream that the thief may have stolen from you. The Scripture tells us:

> *The thief cometh not, but for to steal, and to kill, and to destroy: I am come that they might have life, and that they might have it more abundantly.*
>
> John 10:10

God wants us all to live the abundant life, to walk in prosperity and live in His absolute best at all times. Why, then, does it seem that some believers walk in abundance while others never seem to?

There is a God (the one true God) who promises to bring us abundance, but there is also a thief who wants to steal, kill, and destroy everything that God has promised us. Satan's goal is to steal our dreams because he knows that if he can do that, he can destroy our future. We have to remember that if Satan can't steal our dreams, he can't take our future! It's up to us to stop him from stealing our dreams.

Did you know that Satan wants to steal your dreams? It's true. You are a threat to him as long as you continue to pursue all that God has for you. If you choose to walk in the abundance that God has promised you, the devil will always try to come and steal away everything you have—including your dreams.

However, you don't need to worry. Although the devil is a thief, you are a partaker of abundant life. Because Jesus is with you, in you, and able to deliver you, there is nothing for you to be concerned about when the oppressor comes.

When we read the book of Acts, we learn that "God anointed Jesus of Nazareth with the Holy Ghost and with power: who went about doing good, and healing all that were oppressed of the devil; for God was with him" (Acts 10:38). Jesus healed all who were oppressed of the devil—*all!* That includes you.

If Satan is challenging and oppressing you, it doesn't mean defeat. It could be a clear sign that you are doing something that is making him afraid.

Notice I said that Satan is afraid, not you. The devil wants to stop you because he is afraid if you win, then the more you will talk about his defeat.

One of the methods the devil uses to steal the dreams of the believer is to lie. The Bible tells us that Satan abides "…not in the truth, because there is no truth in him. When he speaketh a lie, he speaketh of his own: for he is a liar, and the father of it" (John 8:44).

Satan is the father of lies. That means everything he says to you is a lie. When he tells you that you will never see a financial breakthrough in your life, it is a lie. When he tells you that you cannot be healed, it is a lie. When he tells you that you will never fulfill your dreams, it is a lie. In fact, John 8:44 is *proof* that these are lies.

Furthermore, the same Bible that tells you that Satan is the father of lies also tells you that God *cannot* lie! Paul spoke of this in Titus:

> *Paul, a servant of God, and an apostle of Jesus Christ, according to the faith of God's elect, and the acknowledging of the truth which is after godliness;*
>
> *In hope of eternal life, which God, that cannot lie, promised before the world began.*

Titus 1:1,2

Let's look at the entire truth of this matter. The Bible says that Satan is the father of lies. The Bible also says that God *cannot* lie. This means that while everything that Satan says about you is a lie, everything that God says about you is true. If God says that you are healed, then you are healed. (Isa. 53:5.) If He says that you are to live an abundant life, then it is so. If He has told you that He is able to do exceedingly, abundantly above all that you can ever ask or think, then He is. (Eph. 3:20.)

Many believers easily acknowledge that the devil is a liar but forget that everything God says is true. Perhaps you've heard the saying, "God said it; I believe it; that settles it." I have to slightly disagree with that statement. This is the way I see it: God said it, and that settles it! It is settled whether we believe it or not. Our believing it will only be to our advantage.

FEAR—SATAN'S COUNTERFEIT TO FAITH

The advantage of believing is the confidence that is produced when you believe. When you believe what God says, there is no need to be afraid of what the devil says. Fear is not a product of anything God says; the product of God's Word is faith, as Romans 10:17 tells us: "So then faith cometh by hearing, and hearing by the word of God."

When we consistently listen to the Word of God, faith is produced. On the other hand, when we listen to the voice of the devil, fear is produced. The reason is that fear opposes faith. It is the spiritual force that causes Satan to produce the greatest possible damage.

Three words should never come out of the mouth of the believer. Those three words are: "I am afraid." These words immediately put to action the works of the adversary.

That's what the devil wants you to say when you're under pressure and it looks as if everything you're going through is impossible to overcome. The first thing the devil wants you to do is to question God's faithfulness. The devil loves it when Christians start to question God, and the strongest way you can question God's integrity is to say that you are afraid.

The devil loves to hear words of fear come out of the mouths of believers because it means he has successfully gotten them to oppose their own nature. A believer naturally believes; it is unnatural for a believer to walk in unbelief. The most natural thing for the children of God to do is to trust their Father.

Anybody who does not trust one's father either has a father who cannot be depended upon or has believed lies about him. Perhaps you grew up with a father who couldn't be trusted. If that is the case, it would be understandable why you have no confidence in that father. However, your heavenly Father cannot lie. He can be trusted. The Bible tells us:

> *God is not a man, that he should lie; neither the son of man, that he should repent: hath he said, and shall he not do it? or hath he spoken, and shall he not make it good?*
>
> Numbers 23:19

It is impossible for God to lie. He can be trusted. If you're having a problem trusting the Father God, perhaps you need to get to know Him better. Whatever He says will be done. He will make good on all of the promises He has spoken out of His mouth and written in His Word.

Contrarily, the devil will take every measure to lie to you about God. Here is a simple rule of thumb for living by faith: Whenever the devil tells you something, believe the opposite. Everything the devil says is a lie. When he starts saying there is no way out of your current situation, it's a lie. When he tells you God is not hearing your prayer, it's a lie.

It is impossible for Satan to tell the truth. The next time he tells you something, don't cry. Just laugh! He cannot help himself. Everything he says is a lie.

The devil may try to tell you that your children will never get saved. He may say that he is going to destroy your marriage. Those things are lies designed to bring fear into your life to oppose the faith that is in your heart.

According to Hebrews 11:1, "faith is the substance of things hoped for...." Yet fear is the substance of things dreaded. It is important to remember that when God speaks, faith comes. On the other hand, when Satan speaks, fear comes—if you believe what he says.

THE THING I HAVE GREATLY "FAITHED"

Just as you must mix faith with what God says in order to give His Word substance, you must mix fear with what the devil says in order to give his words substance. This is exactly what happened with Job.

For the thing which I greatly feared is come upon me, and that which I was afraid of is come unto me.

Job 3:25

The very thing Job feared came upon him. In fact, the Scripture tells us that Job "greatly" feared. His fear activated the will of the devil. As a result, Job lost everything he had. The same thing can happen to anyone who listens to and believes what the devil says.

If something you greatly fear can come upon you, then it stands to reason that something you greatly "faith" can come upon you. The next time someone asks you why you are living in so much victory, you can tell them, "That which I greatly *faithed* came upon me."

The devil will always tell you things that are in direct opposition to the promises of God. If God says in His Word that you are prosperous, the devil will tell you that you are broke. If God says that you are healed, the devil will say that you are sick. (3 John 1:2.) If God tells you that great peace shall be upon your household, you can always count on the devil to try to bring worry. (Isa. 32:18.) He tells you lies to try to cause you to respond in fear rather than faith. Although the things he says are lies, he wants you to believe them and respond in fear so that substance can be added to those lies.

If you want all that God has for you, fear cannot be a part of your life. With faith in God, there is nothing to be afraid of.

CONQUER FEAR BY CONFRONTING IT

No one of us is born with a spirit of fear. Nor is it something given to us from God. The Bible says, "For God hath not given us the spirit of fear; but of power, and of love, and of a sound mind" (2 Tim. 1:7). If you're not born with fear and God did not give you fear, then someone had to teach you to fear.

I have a sister who is about four years younger than I am. When I was a young boy, I used to notice my little sister crawling into dark rooms around the house. I would tell her, "Don't ever let me catch you crawling in those dark rooms again. It's terrible in there. It's scary!" After a while, she wouldn't crawl into dark rooms—only because I'd taught her to be afraid.

Fear comes by hearing. Some people are afraid of flying in airplanes because they've heard about crashes. Yet cars also crash. Will you stop driving? In fact, people get hurt all the time simply by walking down the street. Will you stop walking? Will you just stay in bed all day? But some people die in bed.

If you keep listening, the devil will back you into a corner until you are absolutely tormented by fear. He'll begin with something that is not even reasonable; then as you start believing his lies, fear will increase.

If you can develop faith, then you can also develop fear. Just as you develop faith by hearing, you can develop fear by hearing. Remember, Romans 10:17 says, "So then faith cometh by hearing, and hearing by the word of God."

Too many people lean on what the devil says and end up being controlled by fear. If we lean on what God says, it brings faith, and faith gives us the ability to conquer everything that comes our way.

I encourage you today to consume your life with the Word of God. Listen to faith-building tapes every day. Read your Bible—not as a religious duty, but as a faith-developing tool to help you achieve your dreams. Spend time in the presence of God. Fear will leave and faith will come.

Right now, you may feel as if you're at the bottom of the barrel. You may feel as if everything you've done has amounted to nothing. You may have been told that you have fallen too far down to get back up. Now is the time to look to the Word and declare, "When I fall, I shall arise!" I don't care how far down you are, you can arise. Get back up and allow God to help you recapture your dream.

2

It's Time To Recapture Your Dreams

Many people have dreams for their lives, but few ever see them come to pass. Will your dreams be fulfilled, or will they be lost forever? The answer will be determined by your attitude. Fulfillment is the result of an aggressive, positive attitude; failure is the result of a passive, negative attitude.

There are three types of people in this world:

(1) Aggressive—people who make things happen;

(2) Passive—people who hope things might happen;

(3) Wonderers—people who wonder, "What happened?"

Determine that you will be the one who makes things happen!

Since you've become a believer, I am sure that God has given you some dreams. You have probably followed through with some dreams and let go of others. I challenge you to give some thought to the dreams that God has given you. Write them down, aggressively pursue their fulfillment, and check them off as they come to pass. Don't just settle for a life with no purpose. Even though it may appear that your dream may never come to pass, don't sit by and allow the devil to steal it from you.

POSSESSING YOUR VISION

When you know that you've heard from God and have received direction from Him, zeal rises up on the inside of you. There's just something about hearing from God: Once you receive it, you can never again be passive about what He has told you to do.

Once you realize that you have authority in the name of Jesus, you will become bold in your stand of faith. Once you find out that by His stripes you were healed, you can no longer remain passive about sickness. Revelation knowledge concerning your right to live in health demands that you attack that sickness with the authority that He has given you through His Word.

We have a covenant with God, which promises that He will take care of us, so we cannot be passive about what is rightfully ours. Likewise, once you find out that God has a purpose for your life, you must go after it! You have to fulfill what God has called you to do. You must pursue His dream for your life.

Acts 3:19-21 says:

> *Repent ye therefore, and be converted, that your sins may be blotted out, when the times of refreshing shall come from the presence of the Lord;*
>
> *And he shall send Jesus Christ, which before was preached unto you:*
>
> *Whom the heaven must receive until the times of restitution of all things, which God hath spoken by the mouth of all his holy prophets since the world began.*

God is ready to restore some things in your life today. He wants to restore everything that Satan has stolen from you, including your dreams.

If you're not winning yet, don't give up! God is not through with you. If you've made mistakes and had setbacks, then just remember that God is the God of restoration.

It's time to recapture our divine destiny. We need to recapture our sense of purpose. If we are not careful, we can lose our confidence that we've heard from God.

It is time to take back what the devil has tried to take away from you. The devil thinks that he can take away what God has promised you, but he does not have the authority to do so. God has given you the authority to possess what is yours. So, don't give up!

PAINTING AN IMAGE

Every dream that God drops in your heart begins with a picture of that dream before it becomes a reality. In other words, you have to see it on the inside. When you study the Bible and you discover a promise from God, that promise is designed by the Holy Spirit to be painted on the inside of you.

Words create images. The Word of God says in 3 John 1:2, "I wish above all things that thou mayest prosper and be in health…." The Holy Spirit will take that Scripture, those God-inspired words, and create an image on the inside of you of prosperity and health coming into your life.

You will begin to see yourself with health and prosperity. Your image will become perfected through constant fellowship and communion with the Holy Spirit. It will become more real to you than what is happening on the outside.

The Bible says, "As he [a man] thinketh in his heart, so is he…" (Prov. 23:7). God's Word is designed to paint images. I like to say it this way: Your heart is the canvas, the Holy Spirit is the Artist, and the Word of God is the oil. As you fellowship with God, the Holy Spirit will paint an image on the canvas of your heart of how God sees you—not as the world sees you.

Revelation knowledge of God's Word paints images in your heart of who you are, what you are, and what you are entitled to as a child of God. That's why God gave us His Word. The Word of God will paint an image on the inside of your heart concerning your purpose.

In Acts chapter 26, the apostle Paul boldly and authoritatively declared his purpose to King Agrippa. He was able to do that because God's Word had been revealed to him.

> *And when we were all fallen to the earth, I heard a voice speaking unto me, and saying in the Hebrew tongue, Saul, Saul, why persecutest thou me? it is hard for thee to kick against the pricks.*
>
> *And I said, Who art thou, Lord? And he said, I am Jesus whom thou persecutest.*
>
> *But rise, and stand upon thy feet: for I have appeared unto thee for this purpose....*
>
> Acts 26:14-16

Jesus told Paul that He had appeared to him for a particular purpose. Jesus has a special purpose for your life as well. Jesus talks to you through the

Word, by His Spirit. He speaks to you in order to give you purpose.

This is why it is important to spend time with Jesus. He has a purpose for each one of us, but the only way to know that purpose is to spend time with Him. As you fellowship with Him, you will begin to have clear understanding of what He wants you to do with your life.

KEEPING THE RIGHT COMPANY

Have you ever seen people who seem to have no goals, no dreams, no vision, and no purpose? These are not the kind of people you want to keep company with. If you're not watchful, they will pull you away from your dream. They will hinder you from fulfilling your purpose.

To create the proper atmosphere for your dreams to become a reality, you must associate with the right people. Don't share your dreams with non-dreamers. Don't share "impossible things" with people who do not believe that all things are possible to those who believe. As Proverbs 13:20 says, you need to walk with the right people: "He that walketh with wise men shall be wise: but a companion of fools shall be destroyed."

Associating with the right kind of people creates the right atmosphere for success. Some people in your life might feel called to convince you that you didn't hear from God or that what you heard will never come to pass. Even some family members may try to talk you out of everything God has told you.

I remember one time when our ministry was involved in a building project and the devil fought us over it day and night. He kept saying that we would never be able to finish the project. I had been invited to preach in a meeting in Tulsa, Oklahoma, so instead of staying where I normally stayed, I decided to get a hotel room directly across from the campus of Oral Roberts University, and I requested a room with a view.

I checked into my hotel room, opened the drapes, pulled my chair right up in front of the window, and sat for hours looking out at that campus. I told the devil, "Just as faith built this campus, faith will build what God wants me to build."

Now notice that I didn't go look for people who would agree with the devil and tell me that it was impossible. If I had done that, it's highly probable that they would have tried to rob me of my dream and pull me down to their level. I didn't need that. I was building something that was impossible. I needed to be stirred up and encouraged. I needed an atmosphere of faith, not of doubt.

Have you ever noticed that the non-dreamers usually outnumber the dreamers? That means you're going to have to be very selective about your companionships. Your determination to keep the right company may cost you some so-called friends. Remember, though, that the companion of fools will be destroyed. If you walk around with foolish people and non-dreamers, you're going to get hurt. They will steal your dream right out of your heart.

Determine that you're going to associate with the right kind of people who will help create a proper atmosphere for your dreams to come true. Don't run around with faithless people. Don't expose your dreams to people who never dream. Fellowship with those who believe and practice in their own lives the reality that all things are possible to those who believe!

LETTING GO OF THE DREAM

People let go of their dreams for many reasons. Many times, adversity and the opinions of others can cause people to lose sight of what God has called them to do. This is why it is so important to possess a spirit of faith.

Paul captured his divine purpose in his encounter with Jesus, who plainly told him:

> ...*stand upon thy feet: for I have appeared unto thee for this purpose, to make thee a minister and a witness both of these things which thou hast seen, and of those things in the which I will appear unto thee.*

Acts 26:16

Jesus told Paul that He appeared to him "for this purpose"—to make Paul a minister. Just as in Paul's case, when God gives you a purpose, He is also the One who will cause it to come to pass. Your responsibility is to hold on to it no matter how impossible it may appear to be.

Every Christian, whether in the ministry or not, has a purpose and a dream. We all have a God-given destiny. The spirit of faith will help us reach that destiny.

I want to challenge you once again to give some thought to the dreams that God has given you. Write them down. Remember to also write down the dreams that you may have let go of. Recapture them so that God can bring them to pass. Determine that you will never let go of what God has spoken to you.

DON'T LET GO OF THE SEEDS YOU HAVE SOWN

The Lord dealt with me about a few things at a time when I had almost lost my motivation to fulfill one of my dreams. I was trying to recover from a number of setbacks at the time.

I was in a meeting one night and the Spirit of God placed it in my heart to give my airplane to another minister. I obeyed Him and did what He had told me to do. At that time, God had promised me a bigger, better, and faster airplane. However, I had let go of that dream when some things happened that resulted in a lot of financial pressure. When you're barely making ends meet, the last thing you want to think about is a bigger airplane. You simply don't need a bigger airplane when you're trying to stay afloat. Buying and owning it is not all the expense; it costs a lot of money to maintain it. This is why I had let go of my dream. In times like those, you don't want God to talk about expanding. What you want is for somebody to bring you some relief.

During this time, my wife and I wouldn't even discuss a new airplane, or anything else that would demand more money. Yet we knew that God wanted us to grow.

It wasn't long before the Holy Spirit began to remind us of what had been promised to us, so we slowly began to talk about it again. We began to speak about our dream in relation to the seeds that we had already sown. We decided that we were not going to allow our dreams to die. We knew that we had heard from God, and Satan was not going to steal our dream. Then, as we aggressively laid hold on God's promises again, we saw a supernatural restoration in our ministry.

I want to challenge you today to recapture your dream. You may have lost it at some time. We're all human. We all make mistakes. However, if you have sown toward the fulfillment of that dream, then don't you dare let go of what is rightfully yours. There is a harvest out there with your name on it. It is time for you to claim it as yours. Don't let the devil take it away from you.

The reason I can teach you about recapturing your dreams is that I've let go of mine a time or two. However, I have never allowed myself to quit. That is not an option to me.

The Lord said to me one time: *You planted your seed for your dream then you let the weeds grow up around it. The seed is still in the ground. It's still there. Now, get the weeds off of your seed. You are entitled*

29

to your harvest. If you'll refuse to give it up, I'll bring it to pass.

Can you identify with that? I'm sure that you can. If God will bring my dream to pass, then He'll do it for you, too.

REVIVE US...THAT THY PEOPLE MAY REJOICE

The psalmist wrote, "Wilt thou not revive us again: that thy people may rejoice in thee?" (Ps. 85:6). Revival restores your joy. Revival restores the fun in your Christianity. Revival restores the excitement about waiting for your dream and watching it come to pass, even if it's happening little by little.

I remember years ago when God first spoke to my wife and me about going into our own ministry. I was so excited when I formed my Evangelistic Association. I drove to the post office every day with joy and opened my box, only to find that there was nothing there. Day after day I went only to find that no one had written to me, no one had sent me an offering, and it seemed that no one knew our ministry existed.

I'll never forget the day I drove up to that post office and found my first letter in my box. Another minister had sent me one hundred dollars! That offering reminded me that I really did have a dream from God. It caused me to have a greater confidence that my dream would come to pass.

God wants you to have that same excitement. He wants to restore your joy. He wants you to finish your course. The apostle Paul said, when facing opposition:

> *But none of these things move me, neither count I my life dear unto myself, so that I might finish my course with joy, and the ministry, which I have received of the Lord Jesus,. to testify the gospel of the grace of God.*

> Acts 20:24

No matter how things look on the outside, you cannot be moved by what you see. Refusing to be moved by your circumstances is the way that you will fulfill your dream and finish your course with joy.

SEVEN CHARACTERISTICS OF A GOD-GIVEN DREAM

Let's take a look at the life of Moses and see what his God-given dream produced in him.

> *And the Lord said, I have surely seen the affliction of my people which are in Egypt, and have heard their cry by reason of their taskmasters; for I know their sorrows;*

> *And I am come down to deliver them out of the hand of the Egyptians, and to bring them up out of that land unto a good land and a large,*

31

unto a land flowing with milk and honey; unto the place of the Canaanites, and the Hittites, and the Amorites, and the Perizzites, and the Hivites, and the Jebusites.

Now therefore, behold, the cry of the children of Israel is come unto me: and I have also seen the oppression wherewith the Egyptians oppress them.

Come now therefore, and I will send thee unto Pharaoh, that thou mayest bring forth my people the children of Israel out of Egypt.

And Moses said unto God, Who am I, that I should go unto Pharaoh, and that I should bring forth the children of Israel out of Egypt?

Exodus 3:7-11

#1. **A God-given dream establishes identity.**
Moses asked God, "Who am I?" He's seeking identity. God wanted Moses to become established in his identity in Him. Your identity in God is vital to fulfilling your dream. It lets you know that God is the author of your dream and not you.

#2. **A God-given dream establishes authority.**
Exodus 3:13-14 says:

And Moses said unto God, Behold, when I come unto the children of Israel, and shall say unto them, The God of your fathers hath sent me unto you; and they shall say to me, What is his name? what shall I say unto them?

32

> *And God said unto Moses, I AM THAT I AM: and*
> *he said, Thus shalt thou say unto the children of*
> *Israel, I AM hath sent me unto you.*

All the authority that you need to fulfill your dream is in God—the I AM is the One who backs you.

#3. **A God-given dream establishes credibility.** This can be seen as the story of Moses continues in the fourth chapter of Exodus:

> *And Moses answered and said, But, behold,*
> *they will not believe me, nor hearken unto my*
> *voice: for they will say, The Lord hath not*
> *appeared unto thee.*
>
> *And the Lord said unto him, What is that in*
> *thine hand? And he said, A rod.*
>
> *And he said, Cast it on the ground. And he*
> *cast it on the ground, and it became a serpent;*
> *and Moses fled from before it.*
>
> *And the Lord said unto Moses, Put forth*
> *thine hand, and take it by the tail. And he put*
> *forth his hand, and caught it, and it became a*
> *rod in his hand:*
>
> *That they may believe that the Lord God of*
> *their fathers, the God of Abraham, the God of Isaac,*
> *and the God of Jacob, hath appeared unto thee.*
>
> Exodus 4:1-5

Here, Moses is looking for credibility. When you have a God-given dream and you know your divine destiny, some people will ask what right you have to do what you are doing. They may be skeptical of the fact that you are endeavoring to accomplish something well beyond your natural means. They may even criticize you for surpassing their expectations of you. However, when you have a dream, whether you have the praise of man or not, you know you have credibility with God. He is the One who gave you your dream.

#4. **A God-given dream establishes ability.** Moses had a habit of talking about his inability, but when God gave him a dream, it established ability. When you have a dream, then like Moses, you will also have God's divine ability to get the job done.

#5. **A God-given dream establishes courage.** Exodus 4:18 says:

> *And Moses went and returned to Jethro his father in law, and said unto him, Let me go, I pray thee, and return unto my brethren which are in Egypt, and see whether they be yet alive. And Jethro said to Moses, Go in peace.*

After a long discussion in which Moses was extremely honest with God, he finally accepted the dream that God had for him. Therefore, verse 18 tells us, "And Moses went...." The dream established within Moses the courage to do what God had told him to do. Courage enables us to go after what God says is ours.

#6. **A God-given dream establishes boldness.** In Exodus 5:1-2 we see his first confrontation with Pharaoh:

> *And afterward Moses and Aaron went in, and told Pharaoh, Thus saith the Lord God of Israel, Let my people go, that they may hold a feast unto me in the wilderness.*
>
> *And Pharaoh said, Who is the Lord, that I should obey his voice to let Israel go? I know not the Lord, neither will I let Israel go.*

Moses is no longer fearful. He's not afraid to step out in faith.

This is not the same man who had been saying, "I am not...," or "I can't do...." This man is now boldly demanding that Pharaoh let God's people go!

#7. **A God-given dream establishes perseverance.** You will see throughout the story of Moses that he had to continually approach and confront Pharaoh. He had developed perseverance. He had what I like to call a no-quit attitude. He will not give up until his dream has become reality.

God is looking for believers who are not afraid to persevere. He is looking for people who are willing to talk more about what God can do than about what they cannot do. God's divine ability is available to anyone who is willing to take that step of faith to follow after what He has called them to and refuse to quit.

Are you willing to take that step? If so, then get ready to see your dream come to pass.

3
Make It Real

There is something that must be in the heart of everyone who follows after their God-given dream. It is simply this: Your dream must become so real to you that it is literally a part of you. It has to be so embedded within your heart that it cannot be stolen from you.

The reality of the dream inside of you could mean the difference between success and failure. This is why you must hold fast to your dream at all times.

The dream God gives you has to go beyond wishful thinking. It has to become real on the inside of you. Anybody can talk about what they want to do, or what they might do someday, but those who are successful go beyond just talking about it. They pursue it with everything that is in them.

The human mind does not really think in terms of words when it hears something. It thinks in images. When someone says, "dog," you don't automatically think d-o-g. You normally picture a dog in your mind. In fact, if you have a dog, you probably see your dog when the word "dog" is mentioned. If I say, "black dog," and your dog's not black, you won't see yours. You'll see a picture of a black dog. If I say, "big, black dog with curly hair and white paws," that's what you will see. Every word I add perfects the image.

God had the Bible put in print so that you and I could get an image of His promises. When we read it, we can visualize what He has said to us about our dreams. The more we hear the Word of God, the more the image of our dream is perfected within us.

This is what happened with Abraham. God spoke to him, and the more God spoke, the clearer the dream became to Abraham. Originally, he had no idea where God was going to take him. However, in time, it became clear that he was looking for Something authored by God.

> *By faith he sojourned in the land of promise, as in a strange country, dwelling in tabernacles with Isaac and Jacob, the heirs with him of the same promise:*
>
> *For he looked for a city which hath foundations, whose builder and maker is God.*
>
> Hebrews 11:9,10

Even though you may not see it all clearly yet, God wants to be the Architect and the Builder of your dreams. He wants to paint inside of you a picture of your destiny.

No matter who you are or what your background is, God has a plan for your life. God is not just going around picking out a few people and dropping dreams in their hearts because He loves them more than He loves someone else.

God wants to plant dreams in the hearts of every one of His children. However, in order for a dream to drop into your heart, you've got to be in communion with Him. You've got to have time and fellowship with Him.

As a result, you'll begin to anticipate the fulfillment of that dream. You'll begin to expect it to come to pass. If it doesn't come to pass tomorrow, you will look for it the next day. If it doesn't come to pass this week, you will anticipate its coming to pass next week. If it doesn't come next week, there's always next month. No matter how long it takes, you'll keep looking for it because you know that it came from God.

Most Christians have something in their hearts from God that they are excited about. It may be a business or a ministry. They get excited about it and endeavor to make it happen, but then everything seems to go wrong. Then, others start telling them that it will never come to pass. If they're not determined in the face of opposition, they will begin to look for opportunities to give up on their dreams.

Like Abraham, we must be completely convinced that what is in our heart has been designed by God. Every step Abraham took came with the resolve that God was the Builder of the dream. We must pursue our dreams with that same resolve.

Every dream that God has placed in your heart begins as an image before it becomes a reality. God plants these images in your heart like seeds. We can see this in Hebrews 11:13 (NASB): "All these died in faith, without receiving the promises, but having seen them…." Notice these people died in faith, not having obtained the promises, but they saw them on the inside of them.

In other words, their dream was so real on the inside of them that they could see it even though they never experienced its total fulfillment. It was "afar off," as verse 13 (KJV) says, but they could see it. It became so vivid on the inside that it was more real to them than what they could see on the outside.

What was on the inside of them motivated them. It compelled them to go forward and to go beyond what other people were willing to do. Have you ever seen someone who would never give up? What do you think motivates people like that? They see things other people don't see. They have something on the inside of them that propels them forward. They see their dream slowly becoming reality and they are willing to keep marching toward it, even if they may die before obtaining it.

Are you willing to pursue your dream today? Will you give up too quickly, or will you keep on keeping on? Do we let people talk us out of it?

We have to constantly feed our spirit the Word of God in order to stay strong. Under no circumstances should we ever give up, waver, or compromise. As believers, we are to never give up, even if things look impossible.

We are people of faith, and faith sees the impossible as attainable. As believers, we should be willing to go any distance, even giving our lives, to hold fast to the dream that God has dropped into our heart. When we are that determined, then God sees to it that it will come to pass.

God gave Abraham a dream, and he would not give up until that dream became a reality. Hebrews 11:24-27 says that Moses had that same no-quit attitude.

By faith Moses, when he was come to years, refused to be called the son of Pharaoh's daughter;

41

Choosing rather to suffer affliction with the people of God, than to enjoy the pleasures of sin for a season;

Esteeming the reproach of Christ greater riches than the treasures in Egypt: for he had respect unto the recompence of the reward.

By faith he forsook Egypt, not fearing the wrath of the king: for he endured, as seeing him who is invisible.

Notice what motivated Moses. He saw things that other people couldn't see. He was willing to suffer reproach rather than compromise his dream. He was willing to endure the hardest of circumstances rather than look for the easy way out. Moses was looking for that which God had dropped in his heart. He anticipated its coming to pass. He would not allow anything to cause his dream to be stolen.

Look at the words used to describe the determination of these people to hold fast to that which God had dropped in their heart.

Through faith he kept the passover, and the sprinkling of blood, lest he that destroyed the first-born should touch them.

By faith they passed through the Red sea as by dry land: which the Egyptians assaying to do were drowned.

Hebrews 11:28,29

42

Pay close attention to the terminology "kept" and "passed through." When you have a dream from God, you've got to be willing to keep it. You've got to be willing to pass through some things.

Before the dream comes to pass, you may have to pass through some obstacles. Notice that Moses was willing to pass through adversity. He was determined to fulfill his dream no matter what he had to pass through.

Hebrews 11:32-37 shows us that Samson, David, Samuel, and others had this same type of determination to pass through every obstacle to obtain their dream.

> *And what shall I more say? for the time would fail me to tell of Gedeon, and of Barak, and of Samson, and of Jephthae; of David also, and Samuel, and of the prophets:*
>
> *Who through faith subdued kingdoms, wrought righteousness, obtained promises, stopped the mouths of lions,*
>
> *Quenched the violence of fire, escaped the edge of the sword, out of weakness were made strong, waxed valiant in fight, turned to flight the armies of the aliens.*
>
> *Women received their dead raised to life again: and others were tortured, not accepting deliverance; that they might obtain a better resurrection:*

> *And others had trial of cruel mockings and scourgings, yea, moreover of bonds and imprisonment:*
>
> *They were stoned, they were sawn asunder, were tempted, were slain with the sword: they wandered about in sheepskins and goatskins; being destitute, afflicted, tormented.*

If you refuse to give up, you will see your dream fulfilled. If you are willing to persevere, then you can conquer and you can overcome. With perseverance and determination, you can obtain everything that God has spoken to your heart.

We have to be motivated by what is on the inside of us. What's on the inside of you right now?

Can you see yourself prospering? Do you see yourself living in health? Do you see yourself walking in the fulfillment of the dream God has given you? If He's called you to the ministry, do you see yourself in that ministry?

Three words that describe the people in Hebrews 11 are "relentless," "unwavering," and "uncompromising." These words must describe you if you want to see the fulfillment of your God-given dream. When you truly desire your dream to come to pass, then you will become relentless, unwavering, and uncompromising. You must take the same stand

44

that Paul took. When things seemingly became more difficult for Paul, he penned these words:

> *Brethren, I count not myself to have appre-*
> *hended: but this one thing I do, forgetting those*
> *things which are behind, and reaching forth unto*
> *those things which are before, I press [on NASB]*
> *toward the mark for the prize of the high calling of*
> *God in Christ Jesus.*

Philippians 3:13,14

"I press on," he said. There was something on the inside of Paul that caused him to press on. Is that "something" on the inside of you? Are you determined to see your dream come to pass? If so, then this is not the time to give up. This is the time to press on until your dream comes to pass.

REMIND YOURSELF

If it appears that your dream will never come to pass, begin to replay in your own mind previous victories that God has brought to pass in your life. I know you've had some sort of victory. I don't care if it's nothing more than having been healed of hay fever or a hangnail: You've had a victory! You have something to thank God for. You need to constantly replay those victories in your mind, and keep pressing on toward your next victory.

When the devil says it's never going to come to pass, start thinking of dreams that have already come to pass. Replay them in your mind. That's exactly what David did when he faced Goliath. He replayed his previous victories. He said, "The Lord that delivered me out of the paw of the lion, and out of the paw of the bear, he will deliver me out of the hand of this Philistine" (1 Sam. 17:37).

Like David, you can rehearse previous victories. Talk about dreams that have come to pass in your life. If it can happen once, then it can happen again. Create an atmosphere for your dreams to become a reality; then when they do, replay them in your mind so as to remind yourself that God is faithful.

WATCH YOUR THOUGHTS

If the devil is trying to torment you, then torment him by replaying your victories. As you do, he will eventually flee from you.

Your life always moves in the direction of your most dominant thoughts. If you think victorious, positive thoughts all the time, then that's the way your life will move. When your dominant thoughts are pertaining to what God can do, then your life is going to move in the direction of those thoughts.

That's the reason the apostle Paul told us in the Word that we are to be selective about our thoughts:

> *Casting down imaginations, and every high thing that exalteth itself against the knowledge of God, and bringing into captivity every thought to the obedience of Christ.*

2 Corinthians 10:5

It's been said that your memory has two files of your past. File number one contains failures and painful experiences. File number two contains successes and pleasurable experiences. Those are the two files your memory keeps: good times and bad times. Your memory will give you whichever one you seem to lean to the most.

The reason many people have so many negative thoughts is because they go to the failure file more than the victory file. If all you talk about is worry, doubt, and fear, then that just simply means that this is the file you go to most frequently.

I want you to see that there's another file in your memory. No matter how difficult things have been, there have been some good times in your life.

You may say, "You just don't know my life. There has never been anything good." Well, I can think of one: You're still breathing. The Bible says, "Let everything that has breath, praise the Lord" (Ps.

47

150:6 NASB). Draw from the victory file, not the failure file. When those painful memories try to come up, stop and think about the times that God blessed you. Think about all the things God has done for you. He has given you salvation. You may have needed healing and He gave it to you. You may have needed a financial breakthrough and He gave it to you. When you focus on what God has already done, things won't look so bad anymore.

Replaying past triumphs and victories is a powerful way to keep you moving toward your dream. If you keep replaying the victories, then the dream that you're presently waiting for won't look so impossible. In fact, it will become very clear that victory is on the way.

Don't give another thought to the failures of the past. Don't talk about them. Don't give place to them. Forget those things that are in the past. Let go of them, and focus on the future.

The negative things of the past will not build and develop the faith of God on the inside of you. If the things of the past attempt to destroy your confidence, then you must regard them as worthless, and the Bible tells us what to do with worthless things: "I will set no worthless thing before my eyes…" (Ps. 101:3 NASB). The rest of that verse goes on to say, "…I hate the work of those who fall away; it shall not fasten its grip on me."

Bad memories and unpleasant experiences are worthless. There's not a thing you can do to change them. They are in the past. You must let them go because they are designed to fasten a grip on you, to seize you, to capture you, and to cause you to let go of your dream.

FOUR THINGS YOU MUST DO TO ESTABLISH YOUR DREAM

If you are going to create an atmosphere for your dreams to become a reality, you not only must let go of the past. You must also take four vital steps: (1) write down your dream, (2) communicate with God about your dream, (3) give into the dreams of others, and (4) spend time with other dreamers.

Write the Dream

You need to know where you're going so you can set your goals for getting there. Therefore, you will have to write your dream and make it plain. Habakkuk tells us:

> And the Lord answered me, and said, Write the vision, and make it plain upon tables, that he may run that readeth it.

> *For the vision is yet for an appointed time, but at the end it shall speak, and not lie: though it tarry, wait for it; because it will surely come, it will not tarry.*

Habakkuk 2:2,3

"Write the vision, and make it plain." I don't believe God put that in the Bible for us to overlook. You've got to know where you're going.

Every time you read the vision that God has put in your heart, it enables you to run with it. It keeps you focused. It motivates you. It propels you forward.

What is the dream that God has put in your heart? What has God told you to do? What is the thing that causes you to be motivated, causes you to look forward to rising up each and every new day? What is it that puts a dance in your step and a smile on your face? Write it down and keep it before your eyes.

Communicate With God

God has a plan for your dream to become a reality. If you're going to hear the plan, you've got to communicate with God. You've got to shut yourself away into a quiet place to pray and to listen to Him.

I learned something from a friend of mine many years ago. He said, "Tranquility produces creativity." He said, "Surround yourself with things that bring peace to you. When you do, you'll always be creative. If you like flowers or trees, plant them everywhere. Then when you walk in your yard, there will be tranquility, and it will cause creativity."

Find the place in your house that surrounds you with the greatest amount of peace and tranquility. Once you find it, seek God there. Make this your private place to commune with God.

Sow Into the Dreams of Others

One of the most important things you can do in order to see your vision come to pass is to be a giver. Your dream will never come to pass until you're willing to sow into the dreams of another. Get involved in somebody else's dream and God will get involved with yours.

In order to possess something that you do not have, you have to be willing to plant something that you do have. If you want to possess your dream, you have to sow toward it. That's the principle that the farmer operates on. If a farmer desires a harvest of corn, he must be willing to plant the seeds that he has.

Your dream will never come to pass until you sow toward that dream. Get involved in somebody else's dream: Sow into it. Every seed produces after its own kind. If you help to make somebody else's dream come to pass, God will see to it that others will get involved in your dream.

Talk to Other Dreamers

There will always be somebody who will try to talk you out of your dream. The dreamer is motivated by their dream more than anybody else. That's the reason it's almost impossible to communicate it to some people. Not everyone is a dreamer.

Talking to other dreamers can be faith-building. It can help you to learn more about where you are in relation to your dream. When you speak to other dreamers who have stepped out in faith, then you realize that you are not alone. When you speak to other dreamers, their faith-filled words will help motivate you to do the impossible.

Dreamers know that God will give them ability beyond their own ability to accomplish their dream. These are the kind of people that you want to talk to about your dreams.

Doubters discourage you from moving forward. They'll give you a thousand reasons that your dream is impossible to accomplish. In contrast, when you speak to a fellow dreamer, you will learn that there is nothing impossible when you put your trust in the living God.

Despite the words of the naysayers, don't give up. Don't allow the words of negative people to cause you to begin to draw back from your dream. They may even tell you some things that seem to be true in the natural. They may tell you that you don't have enough money in your bank account. They may tell you that you don't have the ability to do what God has told you to do. They may say that you are the wrong skin color or that you don't have the necessary educational background. Despite what they say, don't give up.

Just say "yes" to God. Determine in your heart if God says you can do this, then you can do it. You have the assurance from the Word of God that your dream shall come to pass. Though it tarry, wait for it. It will happen at the right place and at the right time. All you have to do is resist the temptation to give up.

4

Don't Give Up

When you begin to live a life of faith and to follow your dreams, adversity is sure to arise because for the first time you're dangerous to the adversary. As a result of your commitment to follow God, two things will begin to happen immediately.

First, your faith will grow. A major part of following God is to stay in His Word and listen to His voice. Doing this will undoubtedly create a spirit of faith within you that can overcome any opposing force that comes against you.

Second, the adversary comes to steal away all that you have received from God and His Word. Your faith is a threat to the devil. He knows that if you are determined to walk in faith, then there is nothing he can do to stop you from receiving what God wants you to have.

When trouble arises, it is often very tempting to draw back from what you are believing for. However, giving up should not be an option in your life. Although it's often tempting to do so, it will not bring to pass the things that you have dreamed about and prayed for. Faith conquers adversity every time, as 1 John 5:4 tells us:

> *For whatsoever is born of God overcometh the world: and this is the victory that overcometh the world, even our faith.*

Our faith is the victory that overcomes the world. That means that any attack launched by the adversary can be overcome when we walk in faith. There is simply nothing he can do to stop us. Poverty cannot triumph. Sickness cannot stop us. The faith of God in us is greater than anything Satan can throw at us.

In light of all that God has done for us, it is obvious that a decision to give up would mean to walk away from God's best.

QUIT TRUSTING IN YOURSELF!

God can do far more in you than the devil can do against you. God is greater than any challenge that comes your way. This is why we need to look to Him when things are too difficult for us to handle on our own.

If you are in a situation where things seem totally impossible, then you are in good company. The apostle Paul also faced things that were beyond his ability—and he was one of the greatest men of faith who ever lived.

> *For we would not, brethren, have you igno-*
> *rant of our trouble which came to us in Asia, that*
> *we were pressed out of measure, above strength,*
> *insomuch that we despaired even of life:*
>
> *But we had the sentence of death in*
> *ourselves, that we should not trust in ourselves,*
> *but in God which raiseth the dead:*
>
> *Who delivered us from so great a death, and*
> *doth deliver: in whom we trust that he will yet*
> *deliver us.*
>
> 2 Corinthians 1:8-10

Paul wrote, "We would not, brethren, have you ignorant of our trouble which came to us." The reason he wanted them to understand the trouble he faced is that he knew the One in whom he trusted was greater than any trouble. Paul was in a situation that was very critical. In fact, the Scripture says in verse 8 that he despaired even of his life. He was involved in something that was beyond his own strength to overcome.

In this passage, it seems that it is as bad as it can get—until verse 9. This verse says that Paul and his companions "had the sentence of death in ourselves, that we should not trust in ourselves."

Have you ever found yourself in a situation where you knew that you were not smart enough to figure out how to overcome? The first thing you must learn to do when you feel as though things are more than you can bear is to stop trusting in yourself. In fact, the only way the situation will ever change is if you determine that you're going to trust God. Although that sounds like an unfavorable place to be, it is actually the best place to be. The reason being is that it is far better to trust in God than to trust in yourself.

TRUST GOD

You must trust God. We have used that phrase so often that it almost seems like a cliché, yet it is the most powerful thing you can do in times of trouble and adversity. A lot of people say that they are trusting God, but you see them standing there looking sad, discouraged, and ready to cry.

When you're trusting God, there should be some excitement about it. There should be something that rises up in your spirit when you tell people that you trust the God of the universe. You should be happy when you tell people that you have decided to trust the Provider, the Healer, the Shepherd, and the Deliverer. No one who truly trusts God ever loses. No one!

A person who truly lives the life of faith lives an exciting life. To say that you are trusting God is no small matter. Who else do you know who is as dependable, stable, and unchanging as our God?

People sometimes fail to keep their promises. Even if they mean well, it is possible that they might not come through with what they said they would do.

I would never go out and start a project in our ministry because somebody told me that they would do something for me financially, because you just never know what people might do. But I can always trust God. Why? Because He never breaks His Word.

Notice once again that Paul said that he faced a situation in which he could not trust in himself. When it comes to your dream, you have to get to the point where trusting in yourself is not an option. Furthermore, the apostle Paul said that his trust was in God, "Who delivered us from so great a death, and doth deliver: in whom we trust, that He will yet deliver us" (2 Cor. 1:10).

Paul not only declared what God *could* do. He also declared what God *would* do for him. Paul said, "He will yet deliver us." That's where we have to get in our faith. We must learn to declare that God can and God will cause our dream to come to pass.

Notice how these verses read in *The Message* Bible translation:

> *We don't want you in the dark, friends, about how hard it was when all this came down on us in Asia province. It was so bad we didn't think we were going to make it.*
>
> *We felt like we'd been sent to death row, that it was all over for us. As it turned out, it was the best thing that could have happened....*
>
> 2 Corinthians 1:8,9

When you've faced difficult situations, have you ever talked like that? My mother used to have a saying when something would happen and I'd try to make something big out of it. She'd say, "Son, you're making a mountain out of a molehill." I was trying to make the situation bigger than it really was.

That is the way Israel responded to the giant named Goliath. When David found the armies of Israel afraid of Goliath, he was amazed at what he saw. The armies of Israel acted as if Goliath were too big to kill. (1 Sam. 17:24.)

When David saw Goliath, he didn't change his speech nor his attitude. Goliath didn't get any smaller than he was before David got there. Goliath was still just as big, just as bad, and just as mean as before. He was still that same champion of the Philistine army.

Having the right perspective is so important. While the armies of Israel thought Goliath was too big to kill, David's perspective was that Goliath was too big to miss! What do you see when a problem arises in your life? Is the problem too big to overcome, or is it too big to miss?

Notice Paul says in the last part of verse 9 (MESSAGE), "...Instead of trusting in our own strength or wits to get us out of it, we were forced to trust God totally...." When we are forced to trust God, then nothing is impossible. He will come through for us time after time.

There are stories throughout the Bible of people who faced incredible opposition, and none of them ever failed when they trusted God. Even when it seemed as if they would never see victory, God always caused them to triumph.

PART OF THE WINNING TEAM

One of the greatest revelations we can have as children of God is the importance of trusting God. This is the key to overcoming the devil and seeing our dreams come to pass. This is why we must never give up for any reason. We are not part of a losing team. We are part of a team that cannot lose, if we trust in the One who loves us.

When God gives you a dream, it is because He is calling you to do something for His glory—something that will honor Him when it is fulfilled. If He gave you the dream, then it is clear that it is possible to accomplish as long as you do it in His strength. The great men and women of faith throughout the Scriptures had this one thing in common: They knew that they could do nothing without God working through them.

Very often, it is tempting to trust in yourself, yet we all know that in our own strength, our possibilities are limited. In contrast, there is nothing that cannot be accomplished when God is moving through a person who has faith in Him.

It does not matter how difficult things seem right now. God is able to cause you to overcome every situation. He not only can change the situation, but He will if you will just trust Him.

THE GOD OF ALL COMFORT

God is the God of all comfort. Let's carefully look at exactly what that means. Very often, the picture we get of comfort is people feeling sorry for the person who is experiencing trouble. That is not what God does. He is not sitting in heaven feeling sorry for us.

The Scripture tells us:

> *Blessed be God, even the Father of our Lord Jesus Christ, the Father of mercies, and the God of all comfort;*
>
> *Who comforteth us in all our tribulation, that we may be able to comfort them which are in any trouble, by the comfort wherewith we ourselves are comforted of God.*

2 Corinthians 1:3,4

To be a *comforter* means to be one who draws near to those who are afflicted.[1] Notice He's the God of all comfort, and He comforts us in "all our tribulation." God is willing to be your Comforter in life no matter what you go through. He will provide comfort no matter how difficult things seem. He draws near to all those who are facing difficult times in life, and He gives them grace to help in their times of need. (Heb. 4:16.)

God comforts us so that we can bring that same comfort to others who may be facing similar situations, as Paul wrote in 2 Corinthians 1:4.

If you are facing a situation that seems overwhelming, don't give up. God is the God of all comfort. He will provide comfort for you in that situation. Not only that, when it's all said and done, you can impart into others that very comfort which you received.

I WILL RESCUE YOU

Second Corinthians 1:9-10 in *The Message* Bible tells us:

> *...Instead of trusting in our own strength or wits to get out of it, we were forced to trust God totally—not a bad idea since he's the God who raises the dead!*
>
> *And He did it, rescued us from certain doom. And he'll do it again, rescuing us as many times as we need rescuing.*

God says that He will rescue you if you will simply trust Him. Have you ever been rescued in the past? Have you experienced times when there seemed to be no way you could have been victorious unless God moved in your behalf? Just as He has given you victory in the past, God says that He will do it again. He will rescue you as many times as you need to be rescued.

God has a wonderful track record. He has never failed, and we will never fail if we put our trust in Him. This is why we have no need to worry, nor no need to feel as if we should draw back from what He has called us to.

As believers, we must recognize that it is time to move forward without the fear of failure. God has never failed us and our outcome is victory!

When you face an impossible-looking situation, that doesn't mean it's hopeless. That doesn't mean it's all over and the devil wins. It simply means that you are now in a position where you must trust God. This is what you might describe as "where the rubber meets the road," and I can assure you that God will come through.

DON'T BORROW TOMORROW'S TROUBLES

Notice what Jesus says in Matthew 6:34:

Take therefore no thought for the morrow: for the morrow shall take thought for the things of itself. Sufficient unto the day is the evil thereof.

Too many times we focus on the negative. We focus on the things that we have not seen happen but ignore what God has already done. That is the arena that the devil wants you in. He wants you to forget about the fact that you are still called and anointed to do what God wants you to do. He wants you to forget about all that God has already done in your life. Satan wants you to worry about all of the things that you have not seen happen yet and ignore the fact that God is working behind the scenes.

God wants you to focus on what He is doing. Just because it looks as if nothing is happening that doesn't mean He is not doing anything. Even while you're reading this book, God is doing something on your behalf. The angels are busy working for you right now. God is doing things right now behind the scenes that you are not even aware of, because He has promised that your due season is coming.

While you're sitting there thinking that there is nothing else you can do, God is working and He will bless you because your due season is at hand. It could be that before this day is over, your due season will have come.

The devil wants you to worry about the negative things that happened today. He wants you to worry about what might happen tomorrow. He wants you to live your life worrying day after day, week after week, and year after year, wondering whether or not God will do what He said He would do.

Even if things still look impossible and you have tried everything that you know to do, you have nothing to lose when you trust in God. If fact, you have countless, unspeakable riches to gain when you trust Him. So start rejoicing right now even though you haven't seen the manifestation yet.

Paul said to "Rejoice in the Lord alway: and again I say, Rejoice" (Phil. 4:4). Rejoice in the Lord every day, all day long, even when you're facing overwhelming opposition. God wants us to shout and to praise Him.

Not only that, but He wants us to brighten up and change our countenance. He wants us to have the appearance of victory on our faces continually. We do not have to worry about anything. Constant rejoicing will run the adversary away every time. It will confuse him. He will wonder why we appear victorious when in the natural, things look so difficult. He will wonder why we are acting as if the Word of God is still working.

The reason you can have a victorious countenance is that God is still on the throne! He is still in charge of everything. Jesus is still Lord over all that concerns you. You will never turn on your television set and hear the newscaster saying, "We have an important announcement: Jesus has been dethroned." Never! And as long as Jesus is Lord, and God is on His throne, and you have the Word and the ability to speak it, then you can rejoice. It's not over until God says it's over. Furthermore, it's not over until you are triumphant.

When you're under the greatest pressure, don't talk about the pressure. Talk about the victory. Walk around at home or at your job rejoicing in all that God has done. Let the Word of God come forth out of your mouth. Walk in excitement regarding all that God has done in your life. Rejoice always! Spin around, leap, and shout about the victory that is about to come to pass in your life.

Can you imagine laughing in the face of adversity and constantly declaring victory in your life? Imagine the confusion on the face of the devil when he gives you his best shot and you continue to rise up every day by faith declaring that you are triumphant.

It is time for us to stop walking around looking discouraged and confused and start making the devil discouraged and confused. You are the one with the dreams and the vision. You are the one whom God has called. The only thing the devil can do is attempt to steal what God has given you, and he can't even do that if you don't let him.

The things we see in this world are temporary. It is God who is eternal. His Word is true. Nothing has changed about what He has said. His integrity is still intact, and it always will be. God's ability is still greater than the devil's ability. Therefore, you can rejoice now because God is ready and willing to change your adversity into victory.

Quit focusing on what's *not* happening, and start focusing on what *is* happening. We have to give our entire attention to what God is doing right now, without getting worked up about what may or may not happen tomorrow. God will help us deal with whatever might happen when those things occur.

BLESSED AT THE END OF THE ROPE

In Matthew chapter 5, Jesus teaches His disciples a lesson on what to do when things get difficult. His words clearly illustrate why we need not worry when things seem beyond our control.

> *And seeing the multitudes, he went up into a mountain: and when he was set, his disciples came unto him.*
>
> *And He opened his mouth, and taught them, saying,*
>
> *Blessed are the poor in spirit: for theirs is the kingdom of heaven.*
>
> *Blessed are they that mourn: for they shall be comforted.*
>
> *Blessed are the meek: for they shall inherit the earth.*

> *Blessed are they which do hunger and thirst after righteousness: for they shall be filled.*
>
> *Blessed are the merciful: for they shall obtain mercy.*
>
> *Blessed are the pure in heart: for they shall see God.*
>
> *Blessed are the peacemakers: for they shall be called the children of God.*

> Matthew 5:1-9

When you are at the end of your rope, you are going to have to set aside your way of doing things and embrace God's way of doing things. When you lay aside your own feelings and your own way of responding to trouble, God will take over from there.

So often we are accustomed to being anxious when trouble comes, but these Scriptures clearly show us that when we trust in God and become meek, humble, pure in heart, merciful, and hungry for His righteousness, God takes over and moves beyond our ability. Notice how these verses read in *The Message* Bible translation:

> *You're blessed when you feel you've lost what is most dear to you. Only then can you be embraced by the One most dear to you.*
>
> *You're blessed when you're content with just who you are—no more, no less. That's the moment you find yourselves proud owners of everything that can't be bought.*

You're blessed when you've worked up a good appetite for God. He's food and drink in the best meal you'll ever eat.

You're blessed when you get your inside world—your mind and heart—put right. Then you can see God in the outside world.

Matthew 5:4-6,8

You will be blessed when you get things in order and begin to have the correct attitude. When you can see God working on the inside, you will see Him working on the outside.

Don't cry about being at the end of your rope. Don't have a pity party over it. You're in a wonderful position. You are now forced to trust God, and God never fails.

Furthermore, Matthew 5:11-12 in *The Message* says you're blessed when your commitment to God provokes persecution.

…count yourselves blessed every time people put you down or throw you out or speak lies about you to discredit me. What it means is that the truth is too close for comfort and they are very uncomfortable.

You can be glad when that happens—give a cheer, even!—for though they don't like it, I do! And all of heaven applauds. And know that you are in good company. My prophets and witnesses have always gotten into this kind of trouble.

71

God says that you're blessed if you're at the end of your rope and people persecute you and speak badly of you. If they think you're a fool for standing on the Word of God and following His will, don't worry about it. You're in good company. A lot of people have been in similar situations and continued to trust Him. Rejoice when you say that you are trusting God. The same victory that others have seen over and over again in the past will happen for you. The same faith that Paul had to use is the same faith that is on the inside of you. The same God upon whom David depended, lives inside of you.

When you are in a position where you must trust God, He will come through. There will be less of you involved and more of God. And God never fails.

GET AWAY WITH JESUS

God has a way out of every situation that Satan has created to destroy you. First Corinthians 10:13 says:

> *There hath no temptation taken you but such as is common to man: but God is faithful, who will not suffer you to be tempted above that ye are able; but will with the temptation also make a way to escape, that ye may be able to bear it.*

You've got to be sensitive to the Spirit of God in order for you to hear the instructions regarding the way of escape. You cannot keep company with a lot of carnal-minded people all the time, watch television all day, and worry about tomorrow, and expect to get out of the mess that you are in. You have to create an atmosphere that will build your faith, not tear it down. You have to place yourself in a position where you can hear the instructions of God so He can show you the way out.

The Bible tells us:

> *Come unto me, all ye that labour and are heavy laden, and I will give you rest.*
>
> *Take my yoke upon you, and learn of me; for I am meek and lowly in heart: and ye shall find rest unto your souls.*
>
> *For my yoke is easy, and my burden is light.*
>
> Matthew 11:28-30

If you're feeling weighed down and tired of the fight, then get away with Jesus. The solution isn't to watch more television or find another source of entertainment. Too often we run to everything but the solution. Television may seem to give you some temporary relief, but when you turn the television off, worry comes right back into your living room. During all of that time watching television, you could have spent time with the One who will impart strength into you to deal with all that concerns you.

Jesus was saying in Matthew 11, "If you want real rest, then get away with Me, and watch how I work." He then went on to say, "I won't put anything heavy on you, or ill-fitting. I'll show you how to live freely."

If you are at the end of your rope, then it's time for you to get away with Jesus. Spend more time with Him. When you spend time with Him, don't talk about the problem; He knows the problem. Let Him talk to you about the solution.

Everything you do is exposed to God, so you don't have to major on your problems. He already knows what you're going through. He already knows the pressure you're under. You're not going to surprise Him with anything—so there's no reason to sit there crying about it. Just get before God and say, "I've come to get away with You."

A STEADY STREAM

You can always overcome the overwhelming opposition of the devil, but only if there is a continual flow of God's Word in your life.

Even Jesus faced the temptation by the devil to give up. Matthew 4:3-4 tells us:

And when the tempter came to him, he said, If thou be the Son of God, command that these stones be made bread.

But he answered and said, It is written, Man shall not live by bread alone, but by every word that proceedeth out of the mouth of God.

When Jesus was tempted, He did what we are expected to do every time temptation comes: He didn't focus on the problem, but on the Word of God. He said, "Man shall not live by bread alone...." In order to live above temptation and failure, we need something greater than what we can draw from in the natural. It will take something more powerful than natural power.

The Message translation says it this way:

... *"It takes more than bread to stay alive. It takes a steady stream of words from God's mouth."*

Matthew 4:4

It takes a steady stream of the Word of God. If you are at the point of being overwhelmed, you can't rely on what you heard last Sunday. It takes a daily impartation of God's Word. That's the reason Proverbs says, "...attend to my words; incline thine ear unto my sayings. Let them not depart from thine eyes..." (Prov. 4:20,21).

Great men and women of faith spend time in the Word of God every day. They know that victory always comes to those who put the Word of God first place in their lives.

You may say, "I can't think about the Word of God all day!" Yes, you can. You simply have to stop meditating on what the devil told you and begin to embrace the things that God has told you. It amazes me how people can work and worry at the same time but have trouble working and thinking about the Word of God. If you can worry while you work, then you can also meditate on the Word while you work. All you have to do is change your source of information.

Worry is the opposite of meditating on God's Word. Worrying is imagining what will happen based on what the devil said. It's forming pictures in your mind, based on what the devil said, and expecting it to come to pass.

Meditating on God's Word is imagining and forming pictures in your mind and heart about how God's Word will affect you and change your situation. When the Word of God forms your inner image, then you will begin to see yourself winning. You will begin to expect what you saw on the inside to happen on the outside.

When you continually think on the Word of God, a steady stream is flowing into your spirit.

That's the reason Jesus said, "Get away with Me." If you're on the verge of burnout, then get away with Jesus and allow a steady stream of His Word to enter into your heart. If you don't allow that steady stream of the Word of God to enter in, you will begin to find yourself agreeing with the adversary. This can be dangerous to your dreams. Your dream can be hindered if you allow the voice of the devil to influence your thinking and your decisions.

DON'T AGREE WITH THE ADVERSARY

Trust God to get you over. He will turn your adversity into victory.

When you magnify what the devil is doing, you can't see what God is doing. So determine in your heart that you will believe what He says and not what the devil says. No matter how many times the devil tells you that you cannot win, don't believe him.

> *These things I have spoken unto you, that in me ye might have peace. In the world ye shall have tribulation: but be of good cheer; I have overcome the world.*

John 16:33

It is our job to be of good cheer. The reason so many Christians have trouble being of good cheer is because they are looking at the wrong things. They are focusing on what the adversary is saying and agreeing with him.

Don't agree with the adversary. Agree with the Word of God. The Word of God tells us that even though there is tribulation in this world, we are to be of good cheer because Jesus has overcome the world. If Jesus has overcome, then victory belongs to us. This is what we must focus on when pressure comes.

When things seem impossible, we have to continue to follow Him. We have to move forward with a determination to get where God wants us to be, no matter what the cost. When we do, there is nothing the devil can do to steal our dreams.

TAKE UP YOUR CROSS

Acquiring anything worth having requires commitment and determination. This includes following and fulfilling the will of God.

Jesus said:

...If any man will come after me, let him deny himself, and take up his cross, and follow me.

For whosoever will save his life shall lose it: and whosoever will lose his life for my sake shall find it.

Matthew 16:24,25

Get yourself out of the way. If you're going to follow Jesus, there's going to have to be less of you and more of Him. Matthew 16:24 in *The Message* Bible says:

> ... *"Anyone who intends to come with me has to let me lead. You're not in the driver's seat; I am...."*

Who is in the driver's seat in your life? Are you still driving? Is God in the passenger seat? Are you still trying to make things happen yourself? He needs to be the One who leads and guides you at all times—not just when trouble arises. The Scripture tells us to take up our cross and follow Him. If you let God take the lead, you are certain to arrive at victory.

We run into trouble when we begin to believe that we have better ideas than God does. Our ideas are based upon our own ability. God's ideas are based upon His ability. Which would you prefer? He has never failed.

Someone might say, "But, God, You don't understand." Saying that proves you're still in the driver's seat. Who are we to tell God He doesn't understand? What is there that God doesn't understand?

"Well, You don't understand, Lord. I don't have enough money. I don't have enough talent. I don't have enough ability."

God is not concerned about those things. Gloria Copeland often says, "God has never told us to do something that was possible in the natural, because if it was possible in the natural, then it wouldn't take faith to get it done."

When you tell God, "You don't understand," what you're really saying is, "I'm still driving." God is a much better driver than you are. He is the One who gave you your dreams. He gave you your vision. He knows where you are going, and He knows exactly how it will come to pass. He's been guiding people long before you were born. He knows exactly what He is doing.

When God is in the driver's seat, He will lead you to victory every time. Even when you think that things are absolutely impossible and there's no way of ever getting out of your situation, God knows the way of escape. So, let Him be in the driver's seat. If you will, then you will make it.

I learned a long time ago that when I try to do God's part, God just folds His hands and lets me mess things up. Yet when I let God take the lead, He always navigates me to safety and to victory.

THE DEVIL IS A LIAR

Don't let the devil isolate you and make you think no one's ever been through what you're going through. You're not the first one who has ever been through what you are facing. Neither will you be the last.

The Scripture says:

...All you need to remember is that God will never let you down; he'll never let you be pushed past your limit; he'll always be there to help you come through it.

1 Corinthians 10:13 (MESSAGE)

Think about it like this: Whatever you're going through right now that seems to be utterly impossible does not seem that way to God.

Notice that verse says, "He'll never let you be pushed past your limit." That means God already knows something about you. He already knows what you are capable of. He already knows what kind of fortitude you have. He already knows what level of longsuffering and patience you have developed.

Therefore, if Satan is going to test you, he is not allowed to do anything that God has not already determined that you are capable of enduring. If you're going through something right now that looks impossible, then God has already predetermined that you can make it. If God has already decided that you've got what it takes to deal with the situation, then why would you give up? Why would you quit?

Don't you ever again say, "I can't take anymore." Get rid of that statement. Don't ever say it, because that's a favorite phrase of the devil. He loves it. He lives for that phrase. It should never come out of the mouth of a believer.

Become one of the "rare breed" that refuses to quit under pressure. You've got what it takes to be victorious, and there is nothing the devil can do to stop you. All you need to remember is that God will never let you down. He'll never let you be pushed past your limit. He'll always be there to help you come through every adversity.

If we are to fulfill our dream as God intended, then we have to know that we are destined to win. Once we realize that, there is nothing that can stop us from fulfilling everything that He has for us.

VISION

Vision establishes courage. If we have vision, then we already know the end before we get there. God gives us vision so that we can set our will. Once our will is set, there is nothing that can stop our dream from coming to pass. Remember, God has given you power over all of the works of the devil.

> *Behold, I give unto you power to tread on serpents and scorpions, and over all the power of the enemy: and nothing shall by any means hurt you.*
>
> Luke 10:19

There is nothing that can stand in your way if you set your will to be victorious. Always remember that you are the righteousness of God, and God will not allow you to fail if you are determined to stand on His Word. The Word of God promises you victory. Now walk by faith and show the devil that quitting is no longer a part of your life.

5

When I Fall...

Have you ever noticed what little children do when they fall? The first thing they do is get up. They don't sit there trying to figure out why they fell. Neither do they choose to crawl for the rest of their lives. They simply get back up and try it again.

The most natural thing to do when you fall is to get back up—immediately. It is a part of our nature as human beings. It is also a part of our nature as children of God.

When Christians fall, the devil rejoices and tries to convince you that you will never get up. The devil will keep you down if you let him, so it is vital that you get up. Get up immediately.

A prophet in the Bible named Micah wrote one of my favorite verses:

> *Therefore I will look unto the Lord; I will wait for the God of my salvation: my God will hear me.*

> *Rejoice not against me, O mine enemy: when*
> *I fall, I shall arise; when I sit in darkness, the Lord*
> *shall be a light unto me.*

Micah 7:7,8

I want you to notice how positive Micah was when he faced opposition. He did not allow his difficulty to keep him down. Micah was not one to fall down and to stay down. In fact, he let the enemy know that even if things seemed to be dark and difficult, he would trust in God and allow Him to be a light unto him.

It's amazing to me how so many Christians look everywhere but to the Lord for their answers. Very often, people ignore the very One they need. He is the answer. That is why we have to look to Him when things seem to be getting worse.

Micah said, "I will look unto the Lord." That's the smartest thing that you can do when nothing seems to be working. Keep your eyes on Jesus; He knows what to do and He'll reveal it to you.

God wants us to look to Him. He wants us to stop trying to find answers for ourselves and be prepared to receive as we look to Him. His answer will come, if we'll just be patient. Always remember that God is faithful.

WAIT ON GOD

Micah proclaimed that he would look to the Lord and wait on the God of his salvation. There are times when things happen instantly, yet in my personal walk of faith, most of the time that has not been the case. I've had some miracles that have happened almost as quickly as I could speak the prayer out of my mouth. I've seen miracles at the very moment I prayed for people. However, the majority of the time, I've had to wait on the God of my salvation.

I live between "amen" and "there it is." The moment I pray, I believe I receive. Then I start my walk of faith to reach "there it is." Often, the period of time between "amen" and "there it is" can be long and I have no other choice but to wait until I see the manifestation. Yet I made a decision a long time ago that I will not give up no matter how long it takes.

You might be wondering, "How long do I have to wait until my dream becomes reality?" The answer to that is simple. You wait until it happens, no matter how long it seems to take. What is important is that you make the decision to stay in faith. You will either stay in faith, or you will put yourself through the unnecessary task of trying to fulfill your dream through your own efforts.

What I'm saying is, there is no room for compromise. Notice Micah did not say, "I'll try." He said, "I will." If you're going to stay in faith, then it has to be an act of your will. It's not something you try. It is something you deliberately will to do.

If you tell yourself that you will "try" to live by faith, what the devil hears is that you're not committed yet. What he hears coming out of your mouth is, "I'm not sure that this will work."

Any time you try something, there is always an option to quit. When you will to do something, you leave no option for failure or for giving up.

Micah didn't say, "I'll try to wait on the God of my salvation." He said, "I *will* wait."

We must have patience when we pray. Paul said in Romans:

> *But if we hope for that we see not, then do we with patience wait for it.*

Romans 8:25

You simply have to wait with patience for your dream. After it manifests, you will look back and it will seem as if you really did not have to wait so long after all.

I like what Brother Kenneth Hagin used to say, "If you will prepare to stand forever, it won't take very long." There are a lot of people who aren't prepared to stand forever. They're prepared to stand until pressure comes. They're prepared to stand until adversity and persecution come. They're prepared to stand until someone talks them out of it.

You've got to come to the place in your life where you are prepared to stand forever, constantly looking to the God of your salvation. He is not only the God of your salvation, but He is also the God of the manifestation. Do you truly want to see your dream come to pass? Then ask yourself right now, "Am I willing to wait for it?"

I very seldom know how God is going to answer my prayer, and I learned many years ago to stop trying to figure it out. That's not my business. My responsibility is to believe that He will and to wait. It's His responsibility to confirm His Word.

I really have the easy part. I just have to stay in faith. I'm glad that I don't have to answer those prayers. I don't have to come up with all the money that I need. I don't have to figure out how to heal someone's body. All of that is God's responsibility. I just have to believe that He can and be willing to wait.

My responsibility is to find out what God said in His Word, stand on it, and then wait patiently. When

I wait, the God of my salvation always shows up right on time.

SOLUTIONS TO ADVERSITY

I don't know what you're going through right now, but I can tell you this: If you are a believer pursuing your dream, then you will face adversity. Satan is not going to let your dream become reality without a fight.

A woman once said to me, "I don't understand. I just heard you preach tonight how you had to stand on the Word of God and resist the devil. I watched the preachers on television, and they're always talking about how the devil is fighting them and they have to stand on the Word and resist him." She continued, "What's the matter with you preachers? It seems the devil is always trying to get you guys. He never bothers me!"

I said, "Well, I don't want to sound hard and cruel, but the truth is that if the devil isn't bothering you, then you're not a threat to him."

The devil hates people who are a threat to him. When he attacks you, many times it's an indication that you are doing something right and your mani-festation is on its way.

A lot of times, when we're going through trials and problems, the first thing we want to ask ourselves is, *What have I done wrong?* You may not have done anything wrong. In fact, you may have finally done something right.

Micah said, "I will wait for the God of my salvation" (Mic. 7:7). We rarely know the exact way that God will bring about the manifestation. Yet we can be confident because we know that God is faithful and He cannot fail.

Either the Bible is true or it's not. If He didn't intend for us to live by it, then He should not have given us a copy. If He did not intend for us to be successful, then He should not have promised it in His Word. I've chosen to believe it, and so should you.

If God were to tell us that He would no longer honor His Word, then there would be no hope for any of us. But thank God His Word is forever settled in heaven. (Matt. 5:18.) If you're standing on the Word of God, then the God of your salvation will come through for you. He always comes through. Are you willing to wait for Him?

MY GOD WILL HEAR ME

Everywhere I go I expect to see evidence of the God of my salvation working in my behalf. Micah 7:7

says, "I will look unto the Lord; I will wait for the God of my salvation: my God will hear me." What a comforting verse!

Wouldn't it be wonderful to get to the place in your life that you knew without a doubt that your God always hears you? Wouldn't it be great to know that the God of your salvation is always working in your behalf? Well, He is. All we have to do is believe it and refuse to give up.

Micah said, "My God will hear me." Yes, God will hear you, but will you hear Him when He answers you? Will your spiritual ears be attentive to His voice when He speaks? What if He tells you to continue to stand on His Word? Will you be obedient? Will you wait for your dream no matter how long it takes?

Don't let the devil steal your dream. Your future is not in the devil's hands. It is in the hands of the God of your salvation.

6

I Shall Arise

"I shall arise." The statement suggests an unwavering resolve to continue toward your dream. It is a statement that tells the adversary that you will not give up, no matter how difficult things may look. The greatest people in the history of mankind are people who would not give up in the face of opposition. Great people know how to look opposition in the face and declare that they will not give up no matter how many times they might get knocked down.

When we are following our dream, it is not uncommon for us to be opposed. The devil does not want us to possess our dream. He wants us to think that it will never come to pass and become discouraged.

The only circumstance under which the child of God would have the right to be discouraged would be if Jesus was no longer Lord, and the Word was no longer true, then we all would need to find a place where we could come together to become discouraged. However, we all know that will never happen.

Jesus is Lord for all of eternity and the Word of God shall forever be true.

You may be facing the worst crisis that you've ever experienced, but it's not over yet. You've got to learn how to look at things the way God sees them— and the way God sees them may be much different from the way that you see them.

> *The Lord shall laugh at him: for he seeth that his day is coming.*
>
> Psalm 37:13

Satan's day is coming. You've got to keep that in your thinking. It may look as if Satan has you right where he wants you, but in reality you've got him where you want him.

Even if it seems as if nothing is working, the devil is the one who is in the losing position. He knows that his day is coming. He knows that his time is limited. I've learned that when the greatest pressure comes on me to quit, that's a good indication that Satan just fired his best shot, and if that one doesn't get me, then he's finished.

There have been times in my life where it seemed the more I prayed, the worse things got. The attacks of the devil seemed to intensify.

I'd say, "God, what do I do?"

He'd say, "Stand."

I'd say, "I have stood!"

He'd say, "Stand."

Then I'd say, "But what comes after *stand?*"

Once again He would say, "Stand."

After all of that, I'd say, "Lord, I've done everything I know to do."

He'd say "Stand."

Again, this is what we have to do. We have to stand on His Word. After doing everything that we know to do, we must continue to stand, no matter how difficult things appear. God will not let us lose this battle. You are going to win, and your dream will be fulfilled.

PUT ON YOUR ARMOR

Your responsibility is to stand your ground as a soldier in Christ, wearing your spiritual armor, as Paul described in Ephesians 6:13-17:

Wherefore take unto you the whole armour of God, that ye may be able to withstand in the evil day, and having done all, to stand.

Stand therefore, having your loins girt about with truth, and having on the breastplate of righteousness;

And your feet shod with the preparation of the gospel of peace;

Above all, taking the shield of faith, where-with ye shall be able to quench all the fiery darts of the wicked.

And take the helmet of salvation, and the sword of the Spirit, which is the word of God.

I can remember a time in my life when I felt that I just couldn't stand any longer. I felt as if I had stood for so long that my armor was falling off. When the attacks first started, my sword was sharp, my shield was strong, and all the rest of my armor was intact. I responded to the challenges as a good soldier in Christ. I told the devil, "By Jesus' stripes, I'm healed. My God meets my needs!"

However, after doing this for a long time, I got to the point where it seemed as if nothing was working. I felt as if my breastplate was falling off. My shield of faith was so heavy that I couldn't hold it up any longer. I couldn't even see the enemy because my helmet had slipped down over my eyes!

I asked God, "What do I do now?"

He said, "Stand." Then I heard Him say this, "Son, it's time to rejoice."

"It's time to rejoice?" I said, "What do I have to rejoice about? Do you see me? Do you have any idea what I'm going through? Look, Father. I can't hold my shield of faith up anymore. Look, there is no more space for another dart. My shield is full of darts. I've even got darts in my helmet!"

Have you ever felt like this? If so, it is time to rejoice! It may seem as if you have lost everything. It may look as if you will never get over all the attacks that have been launched against you. However, I want you to notice this one thing: You are still standing, and for this reason, it is time to rejoice.

Although the devil may have hit you with his best shot, you are still standing, and you must not give up. Keep trusting in God. Keep declaring the Word of God over your situation. You may feel as if you will collapse to the ground because of all that is going on around you, but continue to stand. It is time to rejoice! You have the devil right where you want him, so straighten up your armor and tell the devil that you will not quit.

In my situation, I finally straightened up my armor and then God said, once again, "Now rejoice." So, I started rejoicing.

However, suddenly I heard something coming through the breeze. It was not a dart—it was a missile! Satan was no longer firing little darts at me; he started pulling out the heavy artillery!

I said, "God, did You hear that? I thought You said, 'It's time to rejoice.'"

He said, "Get ready and keep rejoicing."

I said, "Why?"

He said, "Son, when Satan starts pulling out the heavy stuff, that's when you know for sure you've got him right where you want him. Brace yourself now."

I braced myself, and when that missile hit my shield of faith it rocked and reeled me, and I thought, *Dear God! This is the worst thing I've ever gone through.*

However, God said, "Keep rejoicing."

Once again, I started rejoicing while I was rocking and reeling. Finally when the dust settled, I was still standing and the victory was mine. Just as the apostle Paul said, I was able to stand against the wiles of the devil. (See Eph. 6:11.)

Perhaps you feel as though your armor is falling off. Maybe you don't even know where your armor is. This is not the time to start stripping off what little armor you have left. This is the time to get it back on, tighten it up, and stand. If you will, then you are about to win!

IT'S TIME TO ARISE

*Rejoice not against me, O mine enemy: when
I fall, I shall arise; when I sit in darkness, the Lord
shall be a light unto me.*

Micah 7:8

We've all had an experience of sitting in darkness. Darkness is the absence of light. The Bible says,
"The entrance of thy words [God's Word] giveth light
[or brings light]…" (Ps. 119:130).

The darkness that I'm talking about is that darkness that comes to your mind when Satan bombards
your thought life with impossible-looking situations.

There is no darkness like the darkness that
comes to your mind when everything seems impossible. If you are a woman, then the darkest dark that
you've ever experienced may have been when your
husband came in and said, "I don't love you
anymore and I'm leaving you," or when the school
called your home and said, "We had to rush your
child to the hospital because he just overdosed on
drugs." If you are a man, then perhaps it was when,
after devoting twenty years of your life to a company,
you showed up for work one morning and they said,
"We don't need you anymore. You're fired."

There are times when that kind of darkness will
try to surround you. It may look as if everybody has

turned against you. It may look as if there is absolutely no one who will come to your aid.

When you're sitting in darkness, Satan wants you to believe it's all over and you have nothing to live for. Many people have committed suicide because they couldn't take the darkness anymore.

Micah said that he went through a time when he was sitting in darkness, but let's remember how he responded to it. He said, "Rejoice not against me, O mine enemy: when I fall, I shall arise; when I sit in darkness, the Lord shall be a light unto me."

That is the same declaration we need to make. We need to stand up and say we will look unto the Lord. We will look to the God of our salvation. Confess out of your mouth right now, "My God hears me; the God of my salvation will come to my aid. I will be victorious, and my God will be glorified!" That is the kind of declaration we need to make in order for us to come out of the darkness that we face.

WHAT TO DO WHEN
DARKNESS RETURNS

One of the darkest hours that I've ever spent in my life came right after my wife and I first started living our life of faith.

When I surrendered my life to Jesus, He became a light unto me. He became the One I wanted to live for. From that day, I determined that I would serve Him for the rest of my life, but then the darkness came. I was just beginning to really live for God. I was on fire, and it seemed that nothing could shake my faith in God.

We went to a church service to hear Brother Kenneth Copeland. Our children were just babies and we had put them in the nursery. During the service a woman came running to us with our youngest daughter in her arms. Our daughter had blood running out of the end of her fingers. I didn't know what had happened.

The woman came up to the front of the auditorium and brought our baby to us. Of course, when the people saw all that blood and heard the baby screaming, fear erupted in the place. I held the baby in my arms and turned and looked at Brother Copeland. I was not only about to find out what I believed, but I was also about to find out what he believed. It's one thing to preach faith; however, it's another thing to live it.

Satan was trying to steal my faith. His motive is always to discourage us and cause us to turn away from God. That day it looked as if darkness had returned to my life, but God proved that He was a light unto me.

With the baby in my arms, I turned to look at Brother Copeland and he stopped preaching his message and walked off the platform and came to where we were standing and laid his hands on my daughter's fingers. He said, "In the name of Jesus, I command the blood to stop and the pain to cease." The bleeding stopped instantly.

She closed her eyes and then laid her head on my shoulder and went to sleep. I had blood all over me. Brother Copeland walked back up to the platform and said, "Let's get back into the Word of God." He just prayed the prayer of faith and went back to preaching.

I took my daughter into the men's restroom to wash the blood off of her. I still didn't know what had happened to her. When I started washing the blood off, I then discovered she had cut two of her fingers off behind the first joint. Now, I don't know how it affects you when one of your children is injured, but darkness tried to come over me and fear tried to rise up in me.

Satan began bombarding my mind, telling me she'd never be normal. He told me that her fingers would always be deformed. However, I remembered the Word of God, and I knew it was Satan who was trying to steal it from me. I remembered the book of Deuteronomy, which talks about the blessings of Abraham. I knew that all of those blessings belonged to me. The Word of God says, "Blessed shall be the fruit of thy body..." (Deut. 28:4). So I declared, "God, this little baby is the fruit of my body, and You said she would be blessed. In the name of Jesus, I believe You will restore my baby's fingers."

My faith began to rise, and fear began to leave. I then heard a knock on the door. I went to the door, and it was the nursery attendant. She said, "Brother Jerry, what do I do with these?" She had in her hands two little fingertips that she'd found on the floor in the nursery. She handed them to me, and now I held in the palm of my hand two little fingertips with nails on them that had been cut off my daughter's fingers.

Once again, darkness tried to come in. Fear started arising again. But I continued to confess the Word of God.

We were advised to take our child to the hospital to get her fingers properly dressed. When we got to the hospital, the nurses were amazed that the baby was not crying with pain. Realizing the seriousness of the situation, they got us an appointment with one of the top plastic surgeons in the state of Louisiana.

When he examined her fingers, he said, "I'm sorry. There's nothing we can do. It got the nail root. It got part of the bone. Those fingers will never be normal. They'll always be short."

I said, "Sir, you don't understand. My God will restore my baby's fingers."

He said, "No, no, son, you don't understand. It's medically impossible."

I said, "Sir, that's where my God specializes—when things get impossible." I told him, "Sir, please understand me. I'm not against you. I'm not belittling you, and I'm not trying to be sarcastic. I appreciate your dedication to the medical field. I appreciate all the years that you've given to studying how to help people and to save lives, and I respect you greatly, but I'm not basing my faith on what you say. I'm basing my faith on what God said, and He says that all things are possible to him who believes."

However, this doctor didn't understand, and he was totally convinced that it was impossible. He said, "All we can do is take a skin graft. We'll take a piece of skin from her hip and cover her fingers. They'll never be normal. They'll never have nails."

We knew that we couldn't leave them exposed, so I said, "You go ahead and do the skin graft. God will do the rest."

He said, "I don't want you to get your hopes up."

He then went over to my wife and said, "Your husband doesn't seem to understand."

She said, "No, sir, you don't understand. Our God will restore our baby's fingers."

He took the skin graft, bandaged up her fingers, and had her stay in the hospital that night.

Brother Copeland had one more service so I went to hear him preach. When you find yourself in a dark situation, that's not the time to run from the Word. That's the time to run to the Word. Why? Because faith comes when you do.

I drove back to that church that night and allowed Brother Copeland to feed my faith with the Word of God. After the service, I went back to the hospital and preached everything to Carolyn that Brother Copeland had preached to me. Now, we both would be operating on the same level of faith. We were trusting God for a miracle.

The next day we took our baby home. Once we were home, we absolutely surrounded ourselves with the Word of God. We didn't turn the television set on. We didn't pick up a newspaper. We didn't hang around doubters. We protected our spirit diligently by staying in the Word of God.

We consumed the Word of God through faith-building tapes and books. When we spoke to each other, we talked about the Word. If people came into our house talking unbelief, they either had to sit down and be quiet or leave.

After three weeks, we took our baby back to the hospital, and the doctor removed the bandages. Much to his surprise, the fingers were growing back. He said, "This is impossible. I can tell there is some growth taking place." He then said, "But they'll never have nails."

I said, "No, sir. My God will restore my baby's fingers."

He said, "Impossible! Bring her back in three weeks."

We kept on reading material that stirred our faith. We continued to pray. We were not willing to have our dream stolen. As far as we were concerned, our daughter was healed completely.

After another three weeks, we took her to the doctor again. He cut the bandages off and screamed, "My God!" We looked and saw that God had restored fingers and nails and they were the right length!

We experienced a tremendous victory when God restored our daughter's fingers. Since then, there have been many times when the devil has said, "Jerry, this is impossible or that's impossible." When he does, I just go to my daughter and say, "Terri, could I borrow your fingers for a moment? The devil's trying to tell me that we're facing another impossibility." Then I'll just say, "Satan, look at this. Years ago, you told me that this was impossible, but look what God did. God took an impossible situation and turned it around, and if He did it once then He can do it again."

When darkness returns, you have to remind the adversary of the victories that you have already seen. Declare them out loud. Tell the devil that the God you serve is a God of victory and triumph.

A LIGHT IS SOON TO COME

It doesn't matter what you may be going through in your life right now. You may feel as if you're in the darkest dark you've ever been in. Yet, even in the darkest dark, there is a light that is soon to come if you are willing to wait for it. The Lord shall be a light unto you.

Matthew 14:25-27 shows us this very clearly.

And in the fourth watch of the night Jesus went unto them, walking on the sea.

And when the disciples saw him walking on the sea, they were troubled, saying, It is a spirit; and they cried out for fear.

But straightway Jesus spake unto them, saying, Be of good cheer; it is I; be not afraid.

The disciples had been told to go to the other side. A tremendous storm had arisen, and the boat was filling with water. The disciples believed they were all about to drown, but the Bible says that in the fourth watch of the night Jesus came walking on the water, saying, "It is I; be not afraid."

The fourth watch of the night is the darkest part of a twenty-four-hour period. Most people think it's midnight, but it's not. It's always the darkest just before the dawn.

You may be in the fourth watch of the night. Your boat may be filled with water, and waves may be beating against your ship. In the natural it may look as if there is no way to go but down, but I want you to notice that in the fourth watch of the night, Jesus came walking on the water.

He always comes in your darkest hour. When you're in the darkest dark that you've ever experienced, that's when you can start looking for the

Lord. He will be there with you no matter how dark things look.

The disciples did not recognize Him when He started toward them. They were afraid. They even cried out, "It is a spirit."

Finally, Jesus said, "Be of good cheer; it is I."

Most people don't recognize God in their darkest hour, because they are not looking for Him. Like many people, the disciples had settled into the fact that it was all over, but nothing is over until God says it is over. God will not say that it is over until there is victory.

Jesus is walking toward you today. He has already set Himself in motion. He's got your miracle in His hands. He's walking toward you, but if you're not looking for Him, you won't recognize Him when He comes.

The moment you think that you are in your darkest hour, instead of saying, "Dear God, it's all over," look for Jesus. He is the Way when there seems to be no way. He will be a light unto you.

MAKING A CHAMPION
OUT OF A FAILURE

God called Abraham a "father" before he actually became a father. (Gen. 17:4.) In other words,

God was calling things that were not as though they were. (Rom. 4:17.)

God said, "You'll be a father!" and as far as God was concerned, that settled it. He was saying, "I don't care if your wife is barren and you're 100 years old. I said you'll have a child. I said your descendants would be as many as the stars in the sky and the sand on the sea shore." (See Gen. 22:17.)

Did you know that right now God is calling you something different than what others are calling you? God is calling you a champion; God is calling you more than a conqueror; God is calling you a world-overcomer. I remember when I first became a Christian. I said to God, "What could You possibly do with me? I'm a failure."

He said, "Don't worry about it. I'm a master at making champions out of failures."

That settled it for me.

God has proven to us that we can make something out of nothing. When everything looked hopeless, Abraham believed anyway. He decided not to be moved by what he knew that he couldn't do, but rather by what God said He would do.

God calls things that are not as though they were. The word *call* in this sense ("calleth" Rom. 4:17) means to summon.[2] In a court of law, someone may be summoned to appear. Once a summons has been issued, the recipient could be legally penalized if he or she disobeys.

When God calls for something, a summons is released in the spirit realm and it now must appear in the natural. Likewise, you must call for whatever God has put in your heart.

Start calling for the fulfillment of your dream! It may not exist now in the natural, but you're calling for it just like God does. You have an image of it. It's real on the inside of you, and it was birthed there by God.

Once you call for whatever God has put in your heart, a summons has been issued, and now it must appear. No demon can stop it. The only person who can stop it from happening is you. How? By getting weary, giving up, and aborting your dream. You must wait earnestly for it. No matter how long it takes, wait for it!

IT IS TIME TO ARISE

Do you truly want your dreams to come to pass, or have you lost sight of them? Nothing can stop your dream if you will continue to trust God. No matter how hard the devil tries to keep it from happening, your faith will cause you to overcome everything he throws your way.

Right now is the time to rise up and seize your dream. God gave it to you, and it is worth fighting for.

Satan does not have the power to steal your dream. He cannot take your dream if you won't allow him. When he comes, remind him that you have authority over him. Remind him that there is nothing he can do to stop you from fulfilling your dream. Remind him that the Lord is a light unto you, and your destiny is in God's hands.

Once again, let me admonish you to never give up on your dream. No matter how long it takes, no matter what kind of obstacles or barriers you might face, *don't give up!* Pursue your dreams with everything that is in you, and always remember that God is on your side.

Scriptures on Destiny

Among whom are ye also the called of Jesus Christ.

Romans 1:6

And we know that all things work together for good to them that love God, to them who are the called according to his purpose.

Romans 8:28

Moreover whom he did predestinate, them he also called: and whom he called, them he also justified: and whom he justified, them he also glorified.

Romans 8:30

And it shall come to pass, that in the place where it was said unto them, Ye are not my people; there shall they be called the children of the living God.

Romans 9:26

Let every man abide in the same calling wherein he was called.

1 Corinthians 7:20

Whereunto he called you by our gospel, to the obtaining of the glory of our Lord Jesus Christ.

2 Thessalonians 2:14

Who hath saved us, and called us with an holy calling, not according to our works, but according to his own purpose and grace, which was given us in Christ Jesus before the world began.

2 Timothy 1:9

For the gifts and calling of God are without repentance.

Romans 11:29

Brethren, I count not myself to have apprehended: but this one thing I do, forgetting those things which are behind, and reaching forth unto those things which are before,

I press toward the mark for the prize of the high calling of God in Christ Jesus.

Philippians 3:13,14

God is faithful, by whom ye were called unto the fellowship of his Son Jesus Christ our Lord.

1 Corinthians 1:9

For, brethren, ye have been called unto liberty; only use not liberty for an occasion to the flesh, but by love serve one another.

Galatians 5:13

According as his divine power hath given unto us all things that pertain unto life and godliness, through the knowledge of him that hath called us to glory and virtue.

2 Peter 1:3

Fight the good fight of faith, lay hold on eternal life, whereunto thou art also called, and hast professed a good profession before many witnesses.

1 Timothy 6:12

Wherefore the rather, brethren, give diligence to make your calling and election sure: for if ye do these things, ye shall never fall.

2 Peter 1:10

Blessed be the God and Father of our Lord Jesus Christ, who hath blessed us with all spiritual blessings in heavenly places in Christ:

According as he hath chosen us in him before the foundation of the world, that we should be holy and without blame before him in love:

Having predestinated us unto the adoption of children by Jesus Christ to himself, according to the good pleasure of his will.

Ephesians 1:3-5

For I know the thoughts that I think toward you, saith the Lord, thoughts of peace, and not of evil, to give you an expected end.

Jeremiah 29:11

Wherefore, holy brethren, partakers of the heavenly calling, consider the Apostle and High Priest of our profession, Christ Jesus.

Hebrews 3:1

Wherefore seeing we also are compassed about with so great a cloud of witnesses, let us lay aside every weight, and the sin which doth so easily beset us, and let us run with patience the race that is set before us,

Looking unto Jesus the author and finisher of our faith; who for the joy that was set before him endured the cross, despising the shame, and is set down at the right hand of the throne of God.

Hebrews 12:1,2

For I reckon that the sufferings of this present time are not worthy to be compared with the glory which shall be revealed in us.

Romans 8:18

In all these things we are more than conquerors through him that loved us.

Romans 8:37

But as it is written, Eye hath not seen, nor ear heard, neither have entered into the heart of man, the things which God hath prepared for them that love him.

But God hath revealed them unto us by his Spirit: for the Spirit searcheth all things, yea, the deep things of God.

1 Corinthians 2:9,10

And to make all men see what is the fellowship of the mystery, which from the beginning of the world hath been hid in God, who created all things by Jesus Christ:

To the intent that now unto the principalities and powers in heavenly places might be known by the church the manifold wisdom of God,

According to the eternal purpose which he purposed in Christ Jesus our Lord:

In whom we have boldness and access with confidence by the faith of him.

Ephesians 3:9-12

...I have spoken it, I have purposed it, and will not repent, neither will I turn back from it.

Jeremiah 4:28

I can do all things through Christ which strengtheneth me.

Philippians 4:13

For whatsoever is born of God overcometh the world: and this is the victory that overcometh the world, even our faith.

Who is he that overcometh the world, but he that believeth that Jesus is the Son of God?

1 John 5:4,5

117

If ye be willing and obedient, ye shall eat the good of the land.

Isaiah 1:19

This book of the law shall not depart out of thy mouth; but thou shalt meditate therein day and night, that thou mayest observe to do according to all that is written therein: for then thou shalt make thy way prosperous, and then thou shalt have good success.

Have not I commanded thee? Be strong and of a good courage; be not afraid, neither be thou dismayed: for the Lord thy God is with thee whithersoever thou goest.

Joshua 1:8,9

For our light affliction, which is but for a moment, worketh for us a far more exceeding and eternal weight of glory.

2 Corinthians 4:17

Thus saith the Lord; Refrain thy voice from weeping, and thine eyes from tears: for thy work shall be rewarded, saith the Lord; and they shall come again from the land of the enemy.

Jeremiah 31:16

Being confident of this very thing, that he which hath begun a good work in you will perform it until the day of Jesus Christ.

Philippians 1:6

For God is not unrighteous to forget your work and labour of love, which ye have shewed toward his name, in that ye have ministered to the saints, and do minister.

Hebrews 6:10

Now unto him that is able to do exceeding abundantly above all that we ask or think, according to the power that worketh in us.

Ephesians 3:20

...If ye have faith as a grain of mustard seed, ye shall say unto this mountain, Remove hence to yonder place; and it shall remove; and nothing shall be impossible unto you.

Matthew 17:20

And he said, The things which are impossible with men are possible with God.

Luke 18:27

Blessed is the man that walketh not in the counsel of the ungodly, nor standeth in the way of sinners, nor sitteth in the seat of the scornful.

But his delight is in the law of the Lord; and in his law doth he meditate day and night.

And he shall be like a tree planted by the rivers of water, that bringeth forth his fruit in his season; his leaf also shall not wither; and what-soever he doeth shall prosper.

Psalm 1:1-3

Trust in the Lord, and do good; so shalt thou dwell in the land, and verily thou shalt be fed.

Delight thyself also in the Lord; and he shall give thee the desires of thine heart.

Commit thy way unto the Lord; trust also in him; and he shall bring it to pass.

And he shall bring forth thy righteousness as the light, and thy judgment as the noonday.

Psalm 37:3-6

Let not mercy and truth forsake thee: bind them about thy neck; write them upon the table of thine heart:

So shalt thou find favour and good understanding in the sight of God and man.

Trust in the Lord with all thine heart; and lean not unto thine own understanding.

In all thy ways acknowledge him, and he shall direct thy paths.

Proverbs 3:3-6

The eyes of your understanding being enlightened; that ye may know what is the hope of his calling, and what the riches of the glory of his inheritance in the saints,

And what is the exceeding greatness of his power to us-ward who believe, according to the working of his mighty power.

Ephesians 1:18,19

Wherefore also we pray always for you, that our God would count you worthy of this calling, and fulfil all the good pleasure of his goodness, and the work of faith with power.

2 Thessalonians 1:11

Who hath saved us, and called us with an holy calling, not according to our works, but according to his own purpose and grace, which was given us in Christ Jesus before the world began.

2 Timothy 1:9

But we have this treasure in earthen vessels, that the excellency of the power may be of God, and not of us.

2 Corinthians 4:7

That ye might walk worthy of the Lord unto all pleasing, being fruitful in every good work, and increasing in the knowledge of God;

Strengthened with all might, according to his glorious power, unto all patience and longsuffering with joyfulness;

Giving thanks unto the Father, which hath made us meet to be partakers of the inheritance of the saints in light:

Who hath delivered us from the power of darkness, and hath translated us into the kingdom of his dear Son.

Colossians 1:10-13

[God will] *Comfort your hearts, and stablish you in every good word and work.*

2 Thessalonians 2:17

But the God of all grace, who hath called us unto his eternal glory by Christ Jesus, after that ye have suffered a while, make you perfect, stablish, strengthen, settle you.

1 Peter 5:10

He that overcometh shall inherit all things; and I will be his God, and he shall be my son.

Revelation 21:7

Where there is no vision, the people perish: but he that keepeth the law, happy is he.

Proverbs 29:18

I will stand upon my watch, and set me upon the tower, and will watch to see what he will say unto me, and what I shall answer when I am reproved.

And the Lord answered me, and said, Write the vision, and make it plain upon tables, that he may run that readeth it.

For the vision is yet for an appointed time, but at the end it shall speak, and not lie: though it tarry, wait for it; because it will surely come, it will not tarry.

Habakkuk 2:1-3

And Jesus answering saith unto them, Have faith in God.

For verily I say unto you, That whosoever shall say unto this mountain, Be thou removed, and be thou cast into the sea; and shall not doubt in his heart, but shall believe that those things which he saith shall come to pass; he shall have whatsoever he saith.

Therefore I say unto you, What things soever ye desire, when ye pray, believe that ye receive them, and ye shall have them.

Mark 11:22-24

Again I say unto you, That if two of you shall agree on earth as touching any thing that they shall ask, it shall be done for them of my Father which is in heaven.

Matthew 18:19

And let us not be weary in well doing: for in due season we shall reap, if we faint not.

Galatians 6:9

Now thanks be unto God, which always causeth us to triumph in Christ, and maketh manifest the savour of his knowledge by us in every place.

2 Corinthians 2:14

But thanks be to God, which giveth us the victory through our Lord Jesus Christ.

1 Corinthians 15:57

Endnotes

Chapter 4

[1] Based on a definition from Thayer and Smith, "Greek Lexicon entry for Paraklesis," *The KJV New Testament Greek Lexicon,* <http://www.biblestudy tools.net/Lexicons/Greek/grk.cgi?number=3874&v ersion=kjv>, s.v. #3874.

James Strong, "Dictionary of the Words in the Greek Testament" in *Strong's Exhaustive Concordance of the Bible* (Nashville: Abingdon, 1890), p. 55, entry #3874, "*paraklesis,*" s.v. "comfort," 2 Corinthians 1:3: "...the God of all comfort."

Chapter 6

[1] W. E. Vine, *An Expository Dictionary of New Testament Words* (Old Tappan, New Jersey: Fleming H. Revell Company, 1966), p. 163, s.v. "CALL, CALLED, CALLING, A. Verbs, I. KALEO."

Prayer of Salvation

God loves you—no matter who you are, no matter what your past. God loves you so much that He gave His one and only begotten Son for you. The Bible tells us that "...whoever believes in him shall not perish but have eternal life" (John 3:16 NIV). Jesus laid down His life and rose again so that we could spend eternity with Him in heaven and experience His absolute best on earth. If you would like to receive Jesus into your life, say the following prayer out loud and mean it from your heart.

Heavenly Father, I come to You admitting that I am a sinner. Right now, I choose to turn away from sin, and I ask You to cleanse me of all unrighteousness. I believe that Your Son, Jesus, died on the cross to take away my sins. I also believe that He rose again from the dead so that I might be forgiven of my sins and made righteous through faith in Him. I call upon the name of Jesus Christ to be the Savior and Lord of my life. Jesus, I choose to follow You and ask that You fill me with the power of the Holy Spirit. I declare that right now I am a child of God. I am free from sin and full of the righteousness of God. I am saved in Jesus' name. Amen.

If you prayed this prayer to receive Jesus Christ as your Savior for the first time, please contact us on the Web at **www.harrisonhouse.com** to receive a free book.

Or you may write to us at
Harrison House
P.O. Box 35035
Tulsa, Oklahoma 74153

About the Author

Jerry Savelle is a noted author, evangelist, pastor, and teacher who travels extensively throughout the United States, Canada, and around the globe. He is president of Jerry Savelle Ministries International, a ministry of many outreaches devoted to meeting the needs of believers all over the world.

Well known for his balanced biblical teaching, Dr. Savelle has conducted seminars, crusades, and conventions for over thirty years, as well as ministered in thousands of churches and fellowships. He is in great demand today because of his inspiring message of victory and faith and his vivid, often humorous illustrations from the Bible. He teaches the uncompromising Word of God with a power and an authority that is exciting but with a love that delivers the message directly to the spirit man.

In addition to operating his international headquarters in Crowley, Texas, Dr. Savelle is also founder of JSMI-United Kingdom, JSMI-South Africa, JSMI-Australia, JSMI-Tanzania, JSMI-Asia, and JSMI-Botswana. He established the Heritage of Faith Correspondence School, and also pastors a church with his wife, Carolyn, in Crowley, Texas, called Heritage of Faith Christian Center.

The missions outreaches of his ministry extend to over fifty countries around the world.

Dr. Savelle has written many books and has an extensive video and cassette teaching-tape ministry and a nationwide television broadcast *Adventures In Faith*. Thousands of books, tapes, and videos are distributed around the world every year through Jerry Savelle Ministries International.

For a complete list of books and tapes
by Jerry Savelle, write:

Jerry Savelle Ministries
P.O. Box 748
Crowley, Texas 76036
www.jsmi.org

*Please include your prayer requests
and comments when you write.*

Other Books by Jerry Savelle

If Satan Can't Steal Your Joy…He Can't Keep Your Goods

Expect the Extraordinary

The Established Heart

A Right Mental Attitude

Sharing Jesus Effectively

The Nature of Faith

Force of Joy

God's Provision for Healing

Victory & Success Are Yours!

Purged by Fire

You Can Have Abundant Life

Are You Tired of Sowing Much?

Don't Let Go of Your Dreams

Faith Building Daily Devotionals

Honoring Your Heritage of Faith

Turning Your Adversity Into Victory

How To Overcome Financial Famine

Leaving the Tears Behind

You're Somebody Special to God

Additional copies of this book
are available from your local bookstore.

If this book has been a blessing to you, or if you would
like to see more of the Harrison House product line,
please visit us on our Web site at
www.harrisonhouse.com

HARRISON HOUSE
Tulsa, Oklahoma 74153

www.harrisonhouse.com

Fast. Easy. Convenient!

- ◆ New Book Information
- ◆ Look Inside the Book
- ◆ Press Releases
- ◆ Bestsellers

- ◆ Free E-News
- ◆ Author Biographies
- ◆ Upcoming Books
- ◆ Share Your Testimony

For the latest in book news and author information, please visit us on the Web at www.harrisonhouse.com. Get up-to-date pictures and details on all our powerful and life-changing products. Sign up for our e-mail newsletter, *Friends of the House,* and receive free monthly information on our authors and products including testimonials, author announcements, and more!

Harrison House—
Books That Bring Hope, Books That Bring Change

The Harrison House Vision

Proclaiming the truth and the power
Of the Gospel of Jesus Christ
With excellence;

Challenging Christians to
Live victoriously,
Grow spiritually,
Know God intimately.